![BLACK & DECKER]

OUTDOOR HO

Fences, Walls & Gates

Entries, Walls & Trellises for Your Outdoor Home

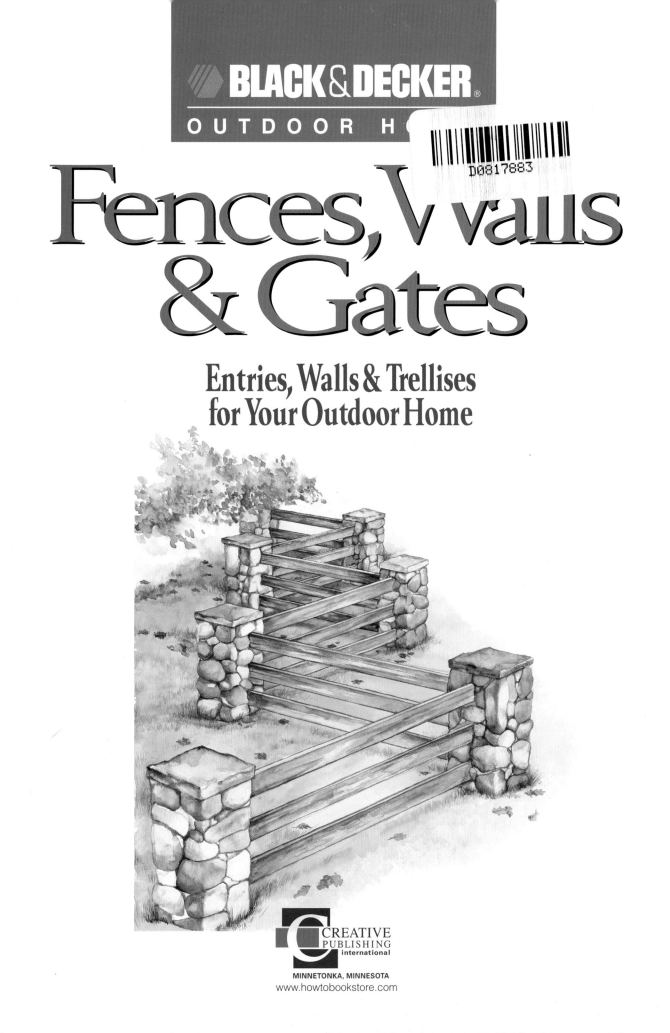

CREATIVE PUBLISHING international

MINNETONKA, MINNESOTA
www.howtobookstore.com

Executive Editor: Bryan Trandem
Editorial Director: Jerri Farris
Creative Director: Tim Himsel
Managing Editor: Michelle Skudlarek

Authors: Jerri Farris, Tim Himsel
Editor: Thomas G. Lemmer
Additional Writer: Ruth Taswell
Project Manager: Julie Caruso
Copy Editor: Jennifer Calliandro
Assisting Art Directors: Kari Johnston, Kevin Walton
Mac Designer: Kari Johnston
Photo Researchers: Julie Caruso, Angie Hartwell
Technical Photo Editor: Keith Thompson
Technical Photo Stylist: Sean Doyle
Studio Services Manager: Marcia Chambers
Photo Services Coordinator: Carol Osterhus
Photographers: Tate Carlson, Chuck Nields
Scene Shop Carpenters: Scott Ashfeild, Dan Widerski
Manager, Production Services: Kim Gerber
Production Manager: Janell Schmidt
Illustrator: Jan-Willem Boer
Technical Illustrators: Earl Slack, Rich Stromwall

CREATIVE
PUBLISHING
international

Printed by R. R. Donnelley & Sons Co.
10 9 8 7 6 5 4 3 2 1

President/CEO: David D. Murphy
Vice President/Editor-in-Chief: Patricia K. Jacobsen
Vice President/Retail Sales & Marketing: Richard M. Miller

FENCES, WALLS & GATES
Created by: The Editors of Creative
Publishing international, Inc. in
cooperation with Black & Decker.
Black & Decker® is a trademark of
the Black & Decker Corporation
and is used under license.

Library of Congress Cataloging-in-Publication Data

Fences, walls & gates : entries,
walls & trellises for your outdoor home.
     p. cm. -- (Black & Decker outdoor home)
  ISBN 0-86573-584-0 (pbk.)
    1. Fences--Design and construction--Amateurs' manuals.
  2. Gates--Design and construction--Amateurs' manuals.
  3. Trellises--Design and construction--Amateurs' manuals.
  I. Title: Fences, walls, and gates. II. Creative Publishing
international. III. Series.
  TH4965 .F48 2001
  624--dc21
                    00-047499

Contents

Welcome

If you're thinking about building a fence, wall, or gate, the process may seem fairly rote to you: decide on materials, pick a style, and start digging holes. When we first began to develop this book, building fences, walls, and gates seemed that way to us, too. But before long, we were excited about the possibilities they offer for turning a yard into a livable, lovable outdoor home.

We quickly discovered that it's easy to build distinctive fences, walls, or gates—projects that create impressions far beyond the ordinary—without going beyond what most of us can afford in regard to time or money. We wanted to design and present projects that would appeal to you as well as give you a foundation of knowledge. And with that foundation, we hope you'll be able to adapt our ideas to suit your own setting and personal sense of style.

Each project in the book includes a list of tools and materials, dimensions, and detailed building instructions, but it's quite likely that you'll need to alter a project to fit your setting. Whenever possible, we've added information or variations that will help you make the necessary changes. Be sure to read the Planning section (pages 8 through 27) and make detailed plans before you get started.

Many of these projects require carpentry skills, and others require some masonry work, but they're all well within the capabilities of a motivated do-it-yourselfer with access to simple building materials and a few power tools. The work is not complicated, but some of it is heavy—arrange help for those tasks.

Building a fence or wall will transform your landscape. Enjoy the process—invite friends or neighbors to help, and have fun. Take pictures—you're going to want to remember this!

Fences, Walls & Gates

Planning

Now that you've decided to embark on a big project like a fence, wall, or gate, we know you're eager to begin digging holes and pounding nails or stacking stone. We're not out to spoil your fun, but we have to tell you this: to get the maximum enjoyment out of your efforts, you need to take a deep breath and make some plans first. You'll be time and money ahead if you determine exact property lines, have utilities marked, consider the challenges of your site and establish the goals of your project long before you gather your tools and head out to the yard.

The first real task is to define the project. Ask yourself these questions:

- What do I want to accomplish with this project?
- What do I want to avoid?
- What challenges do I face?
- What is my budget?
- How much of the work am I realistically able to do myself?
- How much maintenance am I willing to do on this structure over the next 10 years?

The answers to these questions and the information in this section will help you develop a plan for the location, type, style, and building materials for your project.

IN THIS CHAPTER:

Building Materials

When selecting building materials, consider the function of the structure as well as its appearance. Your choices will impact not only the style, but the durability, maintainence requirements, and overall cost of a project. Wood and brick are traditional favorites, but the versatility and ease of installation you get with PVC vinyl and aluminum products make them attractive options as well.

Vinyl products have become popular fence material choices. Many styles are available in a wide range of sizes, imitating just about any type of wood fence or trellis. When properly assembled, a vinyl fence is just as strong as one built from wood. But vinyl will last a lifetime with no maintenance other than an occasional bath with mild soap and water. The initial investment in vinyl is typically greater than other materials, but its durability can make it less expensive in the long run.

Ornamental metal products add a touch of elegance to a landscape. Over the years, classic wrought-iron has given way to fabricated steels and aluminum tubing that offer the same look and feel in a lighter, less expensive form. Maintainence requirements are minimal and installation is a snap.

Chain link offers premium security at a reasonable price. Made from galvanized steel, it is relatively maintenance free. Chain link offers little in terms of privacy or style, but options such as vinyl-coated mesh and color inserts are available to improve those aspects.

Copper pipe is a unique and unexpected material to use for outdoor structures. Intended for exposure to water and temperature swings, it is ideal for outdoor use. Copper materials are inexpensive and available at nearly any home center or hardware store.

Wood remains the most common building material in outdoor construction. Its versatility lends itself to just about any project, from the plain and practical to the elegant and ornate.

The most important consideration in choosing lumber is its suitability for outdoor use. Redwood and cedar are attractive, relatively soft woods with a natural resistance to moisture and insects, ideal qualities for outdoor applications. In some regions, availability may be limited, so check with local building centers before committing yourself to their use.

Pressure-treated pine is stronger and more durable than redwood or cedar, as well as more readily available and less expensive in many areas. Most home centers and lumber yards carry a wide selection of dimensional lumber as well as convenient preassembled fence panels.

Despite an outdoor rating, treated wood should have a fresh coat of stain or sealer every two years to maintain its durability and appearance.

Natural stone is one of the finest building materials you can use. It offers beautiful color and texture along with unmatched durability and elegance. But these virtues come at a price—natural stone is one of the more expensive building materials you can select, and using it can be a challenge.

Manufactured stone is often designed to resemble natural stone, but it offers greater uniformity and ease of installation. Brick and concrete block, as well as glass block, are available in a growing variety of sizes and styles, allowing you to build distinctive, reasonably priced outdoor structures.

Natural field stone

Manufactured brick, block, and glass block

Natural ashlar

Regulations

Before you can even begin drawing plans for your fence, wall, or gate, you need to research local building codes. Building codes will tell you if a building permit and inspection are needed for a project. Some code requirements are designed to protect public safety, while others help preserve certain aesthetic standards.

Codes may dictate what materials can be used, maximum heights for structures, depths for concrete footings and posts, and a setback distance—how far back a fence or wall must be from property lines, streets, or sidewalks. Setback distance is usually 6" to 12" and is especially important on a corner lot, since a structure could create a blind corner.

If you find a fence, wall, or gate design that appeals to you, don't assume that it meets local ordinances. Requirements and restrictions vary from one municipality to another, so check the codes for your area. If your plans conflict with local codes, authorities will sometimes grant a variance, which allows you to compromise the strict requirements of the code.

Another thing to consider as you plan your project is the placement of any utility lines that cross your property. At no cost, utility companies will mark the exact locations and depths of buried lines so you can avoid costly and potentially life-threatening mistakes. In many areas, the law requires that you have this done before digging any holes. Even if it's not required by law in your area, it's truly necessary.

A fence, wall, or gate on or near a property line is as much a part of your neighbors' landscapes as your own. As a simple courtesy, notify your neighbors of your plans and even show them sketches; this will help to avoid strained relationships or legal disputes. You may even decide to share labor and expenses, combining resources for the full project or on key features that benefit you both.

Set back distance

Property line

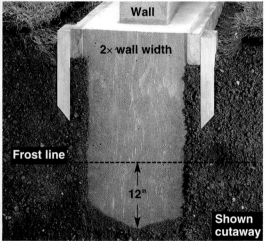

© Walter Chandoha

Wall

2× wall width

Frost line

12"

Shown cutaway

(above) If a structure is more than 2 ft. tall or if it's tied to another permanent structure, it requires footings. They should be twice as wide as the structure and extend 12" below the frost line.

(left) Obey local setback regulations to avoid building any fence too close to property lines, or to a street or sidewalk.

Measuring

Next, you'll need to accurately measure and note the features of your yard on a rough sketch, called a *yard survey* (see below). From this survey, you can draw a detailed scale drawing, called a *site plan*. The sketch for the yard survey can be rough, but the measurements must be exact.

If possible, enlist someone to help you take these measurements. If you haven't already done so, ask local utility companies to mark buried utility lines.

You will also need to mark your property lines. If you don't have a plot drawing (available from the architect, developer, contractor, or possibly, the previous owner) or a deed map (available from city hall, county courthouse, title company, or mortgage bank) that specifies property lines, hire a surveyor to locate and mark them. File a copy of the survey with the county as insurance against possible boundary disputes in the future.

THE YARD SURVEY:

Accurate yard measurements are critical for estimating quantities and costs of materials. To sketch your survey, follow these steps:

Step A: Sketch your yard and all its main features on a sheet of paper. Assign a key letter to each point. Measure all straight lines and record the measurements on a notepad.

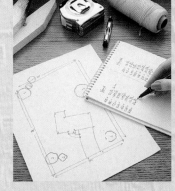

Step B: Take triangulated measurements to locate other features, such as trees that don't lie along straight lines. Triangulation involves locating a feature by measuring its distance from any two points whose positions are known.

Step C: Plot irregular boundaries and curves, such as shade patterns or low-lying areas that hold moisture after a rainfall. Plot these features by taking a series of perpendicular measurements from a straight reference line, such as the edge of your house or garage.

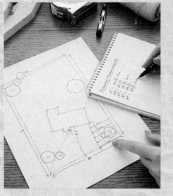

Step D: Sketch elevations to show slopes. Measure the vertical drop of a slope using different sized stakes and string. Connect the string to the stakes so it is perfectly horizontal. Measure the distance between the string and ground at 2 ft. intervals along the string.

Challenges

Planning and plotting a fence line or wall location often involves dealing with obstacles in your chosen path. You may need to get around a tree or rock outcropping, handle a hill or grade change, or cross a depression. You can easily cope with such challenges by removing the interference, or relocating or rerouting your structure. But another option is to incorporate such obstacles into your project layout.

For example, if your proposed fence line crosses a natural drainage path, excavating a swale, or shallow basin (left), allows surface water to flow beneath the fence. If you receive heavy rainfalls, or have dense soil that drains poorly, consider also laying a perforated drain pipe and gravel bed under the swale (below). Take care to avoid directing the runoff into neighbors' yards.

On a hillside, you can step a fence down in level sections, or follow the contour of the slope (pages 21 to 23). For a tree in your path, try adapting the fence to its shape. Install posts several feet from either side of the trunk, then extend the siding to within inches of the trunk to allow for growth. For walls, plot one or more curves to divert the structure around many of these obstacles (page 20).

Dealing with a large boulder is similar. Shorten the fencing above the rock, following its contour, and add a frame to support the shortened boards.

(left) Plant grass, ivy, or other ground covers in shallow swales. Line more sloping swales with stones or concrete to prevent erosion.

(above) For yards with very dense soil with a high clay content or severe drainage problems, lay perforated drain pipe in the trench for the swale.

© Crandall & Crandall

(left) Some designs that adapt especially well to contour fencing are post-and-rail fences, and solid fences using pickets, palings, or grapestakes.

Redwood fence photos, lower left and center, courtesy of California Redwood Association

(left) Board, louver, basketweave, and panel fences are good choices for stepped fences. More geometric in shape, they can also be more difficult to design and build.

(above) You can position a fence close to a tree, but do not attach the fence directly to it. Nails driven into the trunk allow bacteria to enter and promote decay. Wire wrapped around the tree will eventually restrict growth. Even posts placed too close can destroy roots.

Drawing Plans

Good plans make it possible to efficiently complete a project. Plotting fence, wall, and gate locations on paper makes it much easier to determine a realistic budget and make a materials list, and to develop a practical work schedule.

From your yard survey (page 13), create a *site map*, or scale drawing that establishes the position of all elements in the existing site on paper. An elevation chart may also be helpful if you have significant slope to contend with.

On a copy of the site map, locate and draw the fence or wall layout. Consider how to handle obstacles like large rocks and trees (page 14 to 15), or slopes (pages 21 to 23); be sure you take into account local setback regulations and other pertinent building codes.

To determine the proper on-center spacing for fence posts, divide the length of the fence into equal intervals—6 ft. to 8 ft. spacing is standard.

If your calculations produce a remainder, don't put it into one odd-sized bay. Instead, distribute the remainder equally among all the bays or between the first and last bay. When using prefabricated panels, mark and adjust the post locations according to the manufacturer's instructions.

For walls, make sure to plan enough space around the wall itself for footings that are at least twice as wide as the wall they support. Carefully plot each corner and curve, and allow plenty of space between the footings and obstacles like growing trees or low-lying areas where water may collect.

Determining the location for a gate requires a bit of forethought. A gate allows access through a fence or wall into a property, which means its placement is important to its function. Sidewalks leading into the property are obvious gate locations, but consider the need for side yard and service entrances that allow

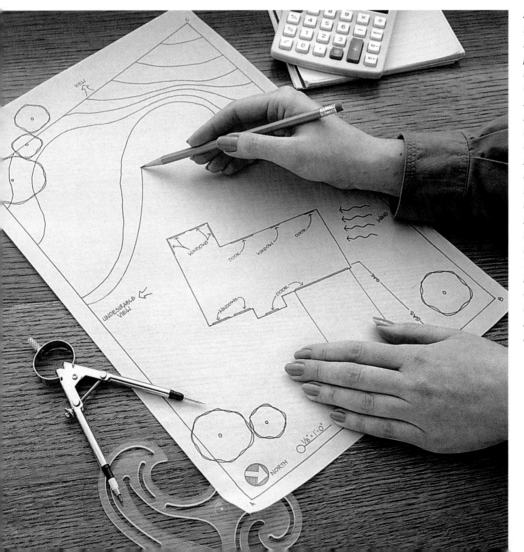

A site map is a overhead view of a fence, wall, or gate setting drawn to scale. It aids in the visualization and planning of a project. From the measurements of your yard survey, convert all actual measurements to scale measurements (if ⅛" = 1 ft., multiply actual measurements by .125; use the conversion charts on the opposite page). On paper, draw straight boundaries to scale. Scribe arcs with a compass to mark triangulated points, noting the edges and corners of permanent structures, such as your house or garage. Use these points as established references to plot all the elements in the property. To finish the site map, draw contour lines to indicate slope, and mark compass directions, wind patterns, utilities, and any other pertinent information that will influence the location of your fence, wall, or gate.

you to bring large items in or out of your property.

Determine the size of each gate, including hinge and latch hardware with an extra 4" for clearance. Mark the size and location of each to scale on the site map.

When your plans are drawn, test them in your yard. Run a string between stakes along the fence line and drape it with tarps or landscape fabric. Look at the mock structure from all sides to evaluate its merits; consider how it will obstruct views and access, and how it will blend with other landscape elements.

Once you've worked out the details and decided on a final layout, convert the scale dimensions from the site map to actual measurements. From this information, draw up a materials estimate, adding 10% to compensate for errors and oversights.

Not every project needs extensive plans and maps, but the more steps there are to the construction process, the more important it is to carefully consider all the details. After you begin construction, changes are expensive and time consuming.

(right) Hang tarps or landscape fabric over a stake-and-string frame to get a sense of the size of the structure and its impact on the landscape.

COMMON DECIMAL MULTIPLIERS:

Using the following decimal equivalents when converting actual measurements to scale measurements.

Scale	Multiply actual measurements by:
¹⁄₁₆" = 1 ft.	.0625
⅛" = 1 ft.	.125
¼" = 1 ft.	.25
½" = 1 ft.	.5

DECIMAL EQUIVALENTS:

Converting actual measurements to scale measurements often produces decimal fractions, which then must be converted to ruler measurements. Use this chart to determine equivalents.

Decimal Fraction	Ruler Fraction
.0625	¹⁄₁₆"
.125	⅛"
.1875	³⁄₁₆"
.25	¼"
.3125	⁵⁄₁₆"
.375	⅜"
.4375	⁷⁄₁₆"
.5	½"
.5625	⁹⁄₁₆"
.6875	¹¹⁄₁₆"
.75	¾"
.8125	¹³⁄₁₆"
.875	⅞"
.9375	¹⁵⁄₁₆"

Laying Out a Fence Line

Once the plans are drawn, the materials delivered, and the tools gathered, it's time to begin the process of building your fence, wall, or gate.

Fence installation begins with plotting the fence line and marking post locations. Make a site map and carefully measure each post location. The more exact the posthole positions, the less likely it is that you'll need to cut stringers and siding to special sizes.

For walls, determine the outside edges of the footings along the entire site, as for a fence line. Then plot right angles (opposite page) to find the ends and inside edges of the footings.

Laying out a fence or wall with square corners or curves (page 20) involves a little more work than for a straight fence line. The key in both instances is the same as for plotting a straight fence line: measure and mark accurately. This will ensure proper spacing between the posts and accurate dimensions for footings, which will provide strength and support for each structure.

© Jan Boer

TOOLS & MATERIALS

- Stakes & mason's string
- Line level
- Tape measure
- Plumb bob
- Reciprocating saw
- Spring clamps
- Masking tape
- Pencil
- Spray paint
- Hand maul

HOW TO PLOT A STRAIGHT FENCE LINE

Step A: Mark The Fence Line

1. Determine the exact property lines. Plan your fence line with a setback of at least 6" from the legal property line. (Local regulations may require a larger setback.)

2. Draw a site map (pages 16 and 17). Make sure it is detailed and takes all aspects of your landscape into consideration, with the location of each post accurately marked.

3. Referring to the site map, mark the fence line with stakes at each end or corner post location, and mason's string between.

4. Adjust the string until it is level, using a line level as a guide.

Step B: Mark The Gate Posts

1. To find the on-center spacing for the gate posts, combine the width of the gate and the clearance necessary for the hinges and latch hardware, then add 4".

2. Mark the string with masking tape to indicate where the gate posts will be installed.

Step C: Mark Remaining Posts

Refer to your site map, and then measure and mark the line post locations on the string, using masking tape. Remember that the tape indicates the center of the post, not the edge.

A. *Mark the fence line with stakes and mason's string. Using a line level as a guide, adjust the string until it is level.*

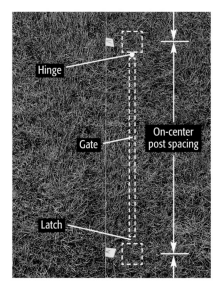

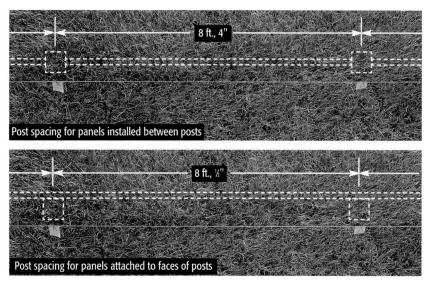

Post spacing for panels installed between posts

Post spacing for panels attached to faces of posts

B. *Measure the gate width, including hinge and latch hardware, plus 4" for the on-center spacing between posts. Mark the locations on the string with masking tape.*

C. *Mark the string at remaining post locations. Use masking tape to mark the center of the posts.*

Right Angles

If your fence or wall will enclose a square or rectangular area, you probably want the corners to form 90° angles. The most effective method of plotting right angles for fences, walls, or other construction, such as pillars, is the 3-4-5 triangle method. Have someone help you manage the tape measures, if necessary.

HOW TO PLOT A RIGHT ANGLE

Step A: Mark One Side

1. Begin marking the fence line with stakes and mason's string (page 18).

2. At the location of the outside corner, plant a stake. Connect the corner stake to the previous stake with mason's string.

3. Plant another stake 3 ft. out from the corner stake along the established line.

Step B: Mark the Adjacent Side

1. Position the end of one tape measure at the outside corner stake, and out along the adjacent,

A. *Stake out the fence line, marking the outside corner of the two adjacent fence sides. Connect the stakes with mason's string, then mark a point 3 ft. along the wall with another stake.*

B. *Position one tape measure at the corner stake and open it past 4 ft. With someone's help, position another tape measure at the 3 ft. stake and open it past the 5 ft. mark. With both tape measures locked, adjust them so they intersect at the 4 ft. and 5 ft. marks.*

19

connecting side. Open it past the 4 ft. mark and lock it.

2. Have someone help you position the end of another tape measure at the 3 ft. stake on the first side. Open it past the 5 ft. mark and lock.

3. Angle the second tape measure toward the first, so that the two tapes intersect at the 5 ft. mark for the diagonal measurement and the 4 ft. mark for the perpendicular measurement.

4. Run mason's string from this stake to the outside corner stake. The 3 ft. and 4 ft. mason's strings form a right angle. Extend or shorten the mason's string, as needed.

5. Stake out the exact dimensions for the rest of your structure according to your site map.

A. *Plot a right angle. Tie mason's string to a pair of stakes equidistant from the corner stake. Plant a stake where the two strings meet, opposite the corner stake, to form a square.*

B. *Tie a piece of mason's string to stake opposite the corner stake, just long enough to reach the stakes marking the end points of the curve.*

Curves

A curved wall can add appeal to an otherwise dull landscape. With a few tools, you can make a simple "compass" to plot the curve symmetrically on the ground.

HOW TO PLOT A CURVE

Step A: Form a Square

1. Plot a right angle, using the 3-4-5 triangle method (page 19).

2. Measure and plant stakes equidistant from the outside corner (X) to mark the end points for the curve (Y).

Step B: Create a Compass

1. Tie a mason's string to each end stake, and extend the strings back to the corner stake. Then hold them tight at the point where they meet.

2. Pull this point out, opposite the corner stake, until the strings are taut. Plant a stake (Z) at this point to complete a square.

Step C: Mark the Curve

Tie a mason's string to the stake (Z), just long enough to reach the end points of the curve (Y). Pull the string taut and hold a can of spray paint at the end of it. Moving in an arc between the end points, spray paint the curve on the ground.

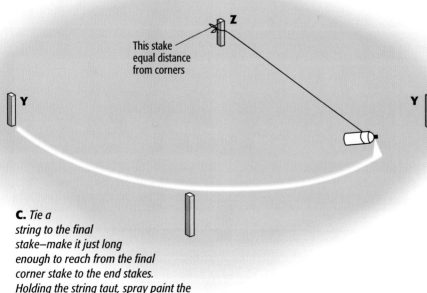

This stake equal distance from corners

Z

Y

Y

C. *Tie a string to the final stake—make it just long enough to reach from the final corner stake to the end stakes. Holding the string taut, spray paint the curve on the ground.*

Handling Slope

It's considerably easier to build a fence when the ground is flat and level along the entire length of the proposed fence line. But few landscapes are entirely flat. Hills, slight valleys, or consistent downward grades are slope issues to resolve while planning your fence. There are two common ways to handle slope: contouring and stepping.

A contoured fence is the easier of the two solutions. The stringers between the posts run roughly parallel with the ground, so the fence line has a consistent height and rolls in unison with the terrain. Contouring works best over large areas of slope, with post-and-rail or picket fences.

A stepped fence takes more time and effort, but creates a more structured look. Each section between posts "steps" down in equal increments, creating a uniform fence line. Stepping works best over gradual slopes. Steep hills or valleys rise too much over short runs, and will cause large gaps between the ground and the bottom of the fence.

Whichever method you use, make sure your posts are plumb and properly set in the ground. If they are not, gravity will work on your fence line and create structural problems over time.

Refer to this section if you need to adapt any of the fence designs in this book for a sloped site.

HOW TO CONTOUR A FENCE
Step A: Determine Post Locations

1. Outline the fence location with stakes and string, as shown on pages 18 and 19. Drive one stake into the ground at the top of the slope and one at the bottom. Make sure the stakes are plumb.

2. Run string between the stakes, 6" above the ground at each stake.

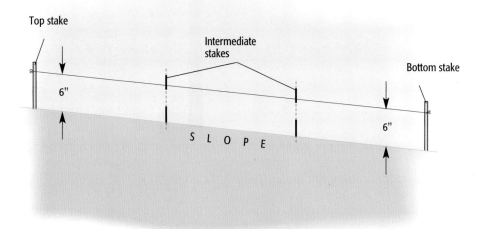

A. *Run a string between stakes at the top and bottom of the slope. Mark the post centers on the string, and drop a plumb bob to determine the posthole locations.*

B. *Mark the fence height on each post, and cut to size with the reciprocating saw or handsaw.*

C. *Clamp the upper stringer at the reference marks on the posts. Scribe the backside of the stringer where it overlaps the post and cut it to size.*

21

3. Measure and mark equidistant post locations along the string, using pieces of tape.

4. Drop a plumb bob from each piece of tape, and mark the ground with a stake for the posthole location.

Step B: Set the Posts

1. Dig footings and set the posts in concrete (pages 24 to 25). Allow to cure for 2 days.

2. Measure up from the base of each post and mark cutoff lines for the height, using a framing square.

3. Trim the posts along the cutoff lines using a reciprocating saw or handsaw. Each post will be the same height, creating a contour fence line that follows any ground variance.

Step C: Build the Framework & Apply the Siding

1. On each post, measure down from the top, and mark a line for both the upper and lower stringer positions.

2. Clamp a board for the upper stringer between two posts, aligning the top edge with the upper stringer reference marks of each. Scribe each post outline on the backside of the stringer. Remove the stringer and cut it to size, us-ing a circular saw.

3. Position the stringer between the two posts and toenail it into place, using galvanized nails or deck screws.

4. Repeat #2 and #3 to install the remaining stringers, both upper and lower, in their proper positions.

5. Apply the siding. Mark each board with a reference line, so each will extend evenly above the upper stringer. If necessary, trim the bottoms to maintain 2" of clearance from the ground. Use spacers between the boards to maintain consistent spacing.

HOW TO STEP A FENCE

Step A: Determine the Slope & Post Locations

1. Drive a short stake into the ground at the top of the slope and a longer stake at the bottom. Make sure the top of the longer stake rises above the bottom of the shorter stake. Check the longer stake for plumb with a level.

2. Run string from the bottom of the short stake to the top of the longer one. Using a line level, adjust the string at the longer stake until it is level. Mark the position on the stake.

3. Measure the length of the string from stake to stake. This number is the *run*. Divide the run into equal segments that are between 48" and 96". This will give you the number of sections, and posts (number of sections + 1).

Example: 288" (run) ÷ 72" (section size) = 4 (number of sections).

4. Measure the longer stake from the ground to the string mark for the *rise*. Divide the rise by the number of sections you will have on

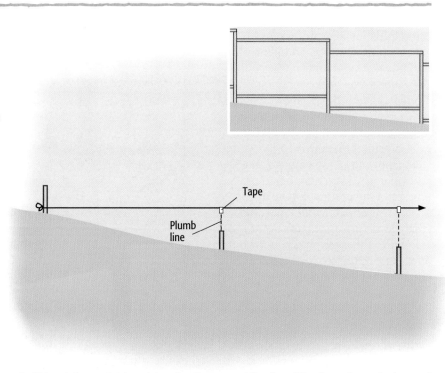

A. *Using stakes and string, determine the run and the rise of the slope, then calculate and mark stepped post locations.*

the slope for the stepping measurement.

Example: 24" (rise) ÷ 4 (sections between posts) = 6" (step size)

5. Measure and mark the post locations along the level string with a piece of tape.

6. Drop a plumb bob from each post location mark on the string, and mark the ground with a stake.

Step B: Mark & Cut Posts

1. Dig the postholes and set the posts (pages 24 to 25). Allow the concrete to cure for 2 days.

2. On the post at the bottom of the slope, measure up from the ground and mark the post height. Cut the post at the mark using a reciprocating saw or handsaw.

3. Use a line level to run a level string from the top of this post to the next post. Mark a reference line on the post.

4. Measure up from this reference line and mark the step size (6" in our example). Cut the post to size with a reciprocating saw or handsaw.

5. Measure down from the reference line and mark the lower stringer position.

6. Repeat #3 through #5 for each post, until you reach the top of the slope.

Step C: Attach the Stringers & Siding

1. Measure across the top of the post to the reference line on the next post. Cut the board for the upper stringer to size.

2. Place the stringer with one end on the post top and the other flush against the next post at the reference mark. Make sure the stringer is level and attach it, using 3" galvanized deck screws.

3. Measure the distance between the posts, and cut the boards for the lower stringers to size. Continue this process until you reach the top of the slope.

4. Apply the siding. Mark each board with a reference line so each will extend evenly above the upper stringer. If necessary, trim the bottoms so they're even below the lower stringer. Use spacers between the boards to maintain consistent spacing.

B. *Run a level string from the top of the previous post. Mark the step size on the post, and cut it to height, using a reciprocating saw or hand saw.*

C. *Cut the upper stringers to size. Attach one end to the post top and the other end flush against the next post at the reference mark.*

Setting Posts

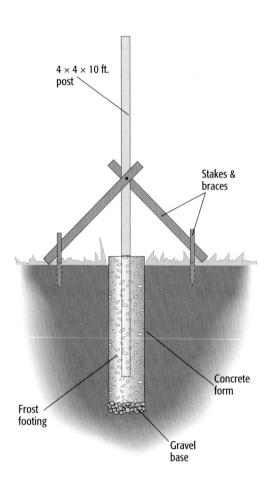

4 × 4 × 10 ft. post

Stakes & braces

Concrete form

Frost footing

Gravel base

After plotting your fence line with stakes and string, dig the postholes and set the posts. It is critical that the posts be perfectly aligned and plumb. Dig post holes 6" deeper than the post footing depth specified by local building codes, or 12" past the winter frost line in cold climates. Good post-setting techniques let you breeze through this process and on to the most satisfying part of fence construction: attaching the fencing to the framework.

HOW TO INSTALL POSTS

Step A: Mark Post Locations

1. Transfer the marks from the string to the ground, using a plumb bob to pinpoint the post locations.

2. Mark each post location with a stake, and remove the string.

TOOLS & MATERIALS

- Plumb bob
- Stakes
- Hand maul
- Power auger or post hole digger
- Shovel
- Coarse gravel
- Carpenter's level
- Concrete
- Mason's trowel
- Pressure-treated, cedar, or redwood 4 × 4 posts
- Scrap lengths of 2 × 4

Step B: Dig Post Holes

1. Dig post holes using a power auger (available at rental centers) or post hole digger. Make each hole 6" deeper than the post footing depth specified by local building code or 12" past the frost line in cold climates. Keep the holes as narrow as possible, usually about twice the width of the post. Corner and gate posts usually require wider footings for extra stability. Check local regulations.

A. *Drop a plumb bob from each post reference mark on the string to pinpoint the post centers on the ground.*

B. *Dig post holes 6" deeper than specified by local building code. Pour 6" of gravel into each hole to improve drainage.*

C. *Position each post in its hole. Brace the post with scrap pieces of 2 × 4 on adjacent sides, and adjust it until it is plumb.*

2. Pour a 6" layer of gravel into each hole for improved drainage.

Step C: Position the Posts

1. Position each post in its hole. Check posts for plumb with a level. Adjust posts to the correct height by adding or removing gravel.

2. Brace each post with scrap 2 × 4s secured to adjacent sides.

3. Make sure the fence line is straight, using mason's string. Adjust further if necessary.

Step D: Fill the Post Holes

1. Mix concrete and fill each post hole, overfilling them slightly.

2. Check to make sure each post is plumb, then shape the concrete around the bottom of the post to form a rounded crown that will shed water.

3. Let the concrete cure for 2 days before removing the braces.

D. *Fill the post holes with pre-mixed concrete, overfilling each slightly. Recheck the post for plumb and shape the concrete into a crown to shed water.*

VARIATION:

An alternative to setting posts in concrete is to use post spikes. Also called post anchors, supports, or mounting spikes, post spikes run between 24" and 30" in length, and are designed with a socket head to accommodate 4 × 4 or 6 × 6 posts. Post spikes with swivel heads help make adjustments during installation even easier.

With no holes to dig or concrete to mix, it takes little time or effort to install post spikes. To begin, put an 8"-length of post into the socket head, and place the tip of the spike on the post location. Have someone help hold the spike in position as you drive it about 6" into the ground, using a sledgehammer. Check the blades of the spike for plumb with a level to make sure you are driving it in straight. Also, make sure the spike remains properly aligned and doesn't twist. Make any necessary adjustments and continue driving the spike into the ground until the base of the socket head is flush with the ground.

Cut a post to the desired fence height, and insert it into the socket head; check the post for plumb, using a level. Drive 1¼" galvanized deck screws (or the hardware screws that came with the post spike) into the pre-routed screw holes, one on each side, of the socket head.

It is best to install the post spikes as you install the fencing. This will allow you to easily maintain the proper spacing between posts and save you from having to cut stringers and siding to special sizes.

Tools & Materials

As a homeowner, you probably already own many of the tools needed for the projects in this book. If there are tools you don't have, you can borrow from friends and neighbors, or rent the specialty tools at your local hardware store or rental center. Make sure you read over the owner's manual and operating instructions for any tools you borrow or rent.

If you decide to buy new tools, invest in high-quality products whenever possible; a few extra dollars up front will cut the expense of replacing worn out or broken tools every few years.

To ensure your safety and prevent damage to your tools, always use a GFCI (ground-fault circuit-interrupter) extension cord when using power tools.

Use galvanized metal hardware and fasteners for outdoor structures: hinges, latches, fence brackets, deck screws, and nails.

Because these are outdoor structures, connecting hardware, fasteners, and materials need to hold up during extreme weather conditions. The better the materials, the longer life of the structure.

Any metal connecting hardware and fasteners, including nails and screws, should be made from aluminum or galvanized steel to prevent rust from weakening the joints.

For projects involving concrete, estimate your material needs as accurately as possible, then add 10 percent. This will compensate for any oversights and allow for waste. Also, make sure all paints, stains, and sealers are suited for exterior use. Follow the manufacturer's instructions for application.

BASIC TOOLS:

Basic tools for building fences, walls, and gates include: shovel (1), clam shell digger (2), mason's trowel (3), propane torch (4), flux (5), solder (6), spark lighter (7), jointing tool (8), ratchet wrench (9), pliers (10), 4-ft. level (11), hammer (12), circular saw (13), chalk line (14), mason's string (15), spring clamp (16), drill (17), tape measure (18), jig saw (19), framing square (20), line level (21).

RENTAL TOOLS (not shown):

In addition to these basic tools, you may need to rent tools such as a power auger, cement mixer, come-along winch, and reciprocating saw.

Materials required for building outdoor structures include: paint, stain, sealer, wood glue, duct tape, cement, rebar, and gravel.

© Bob Firth

Fences

Crawling across a rolling field or guarding a suburban home, a fence defines space and creates a backdrop for the enclosed landscape. Its materials, style, shape, and colors set a tone that may even tell you something about what you'll find on the other side.

Traditional picket fences conjure up images of cottage gardens and children playing. Post and rail fences often surround rustic landscapes or pastures; long expanses of a white board fence can make you believe there might be horses over the next hill. Privacy fences such as board and stringer, or security fences, such as chain link, produce images of swimming pools sparkling in the sun.

If you like the idea of a fence but hesitate because you don't have time to repaint or stain over the years, a maintenance-free vinyl fence might be the answer for you. Vinyl fences are available in many of the same styles as wood and are easy to install. One added benefit: many vinyl fence products are produced from recycled materials.

You might be surprised at how easily you can add some pizzazz to a plain fence. Try building a shadow box bay, adding a framed opening, or building a display shelf.

IN THIS CHAPTER:

Types of Fences

Choosing a fence for your yard entails more than deciding what you like best. Different types of fences serve different purposes—start by deciding what you want the fence to accomplish.

To select a specific style, decide on your main priority: privacy when working in your garden, keeping the kids or pets in a safe, enclosed area, security for a backyard pool, or the addition of a design element to your landscape. Depending on its purpose, such as surrounding a pool, local building codes may dictate some of your choices, so be sure to review the regulations before deciding on a type or style of fence.

Other considerations may include screening out an unsightly view, blocking wind and noise, or protecting gardens or flower beds. Keep in mind that an open or partially-open fence is a more effective windbreak than a solid fence. Wind simply vaults over a solid fence. An open design diffuses the wind current and protects a larger area behind the fence from the force of the wind.

Consider, too, how you want your fence to relate to your site: as an extension of the house, a part of the garden or yard, or a link between the two. Note the scale of your property and gradation. A fence that is too tall may look out of place on a small lot.

© Charles Mann

Wood Fences

Wood fences are traditional favorites. They're relatively inexpensive, easy to construct, and can be built in styles to suit many settings. All wood fences require periodic maintenance.

- Panel
- Board & Stringer
- Picket
- Post & Rail

Embellishments for Fences

Simple, inexpensive ways to add unique character to plain fence lines.

- Shadow Box
- Framed Openings
- Display Shelves

Low-Maintenance Fences

Low-maintenance options are becoming more popular all the time. Some are more expensive than traditional materials but look great for decades with little or no care. Chain link remains an easy, inexpensive way to secure a yard.

- Vinyl
- Ornamental Metal
- Chain Link

Combinations of Materials

Fences made from interesting combinations give one fence the advantages of both materials. For example, using stone pillars to support wood rails adds unique character to a traditional fence style.

- Brick & Board
- Stone & Rail
- Cedar & Copper

Board & Stringer

If you want a high-quality, well-built wood fence, a board and stringer fence may be the best answer. This fence style is constructed from a basic frame with at least two rails called *stringers* that run parallel to the ground between posts to form the framework. Vertical boards, called *siding*, are attached to the framework created by the stringers.

A board and stringer fence is well-suited for yards of almost any contour. Consult the section on handling slope (pages 21 to 23) for instructions on how to adapt a board-and-stringer fence to a sloped yard.

We used dog-eared siding in this project, but these construction methods can be used with many siding patterns (see page 34). Spend a little time looking at magazines and driving through your favorite neighborhoods—you're certain to find a siding style that appeals to you and suits your property.

HOW TO BUILD A BOARD & STRINGER FENCE

Step A: Trim the Posts & Add the Top Stringers

1. Lay out the fence line (pages 18 to 19) and install the posts (pages 24 to 25). Let the concrete cure for at least 2 days.

2. On each post, measure up from the ground to a point 12" below the planned fence height. Snap a level chalk line across all posts at this height. Trim the posts, using a reciprocating saw.

3. Cut a 2 × 4 to 72" for the top stringer. Coat the ends of the stringers with sealer and let them dry.

4. Place the stringers flat on top of the posts, centering the joints over each post. Attach the stringers to the posts, using 3" galvanized deck screws.

Step B: Install the Remaining Stringers

1. Measuring down from the top of each post, mark lines at 24" intervals to mark the locations for the other stringers in this bay.

2. At each mark, use 4d galvanized nails to secure a 2 × 4 fence bracket to the inside face of the post, flush with the outside edge.

3. Position a 2 × 4 between each pair of brackets.

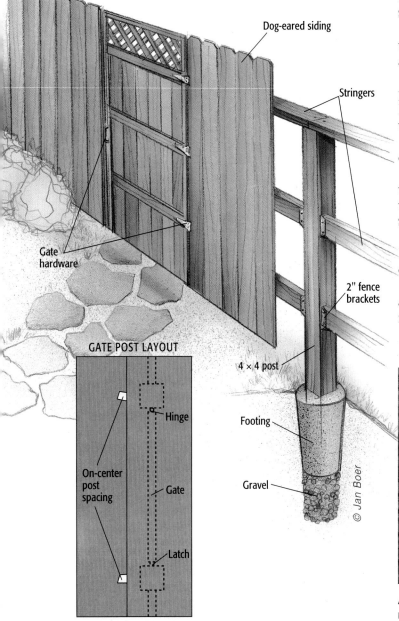

Dog-eared siding

Stringers

Gate hardware

2" fence brackets

4 × 4 post

Footing

Gravel

© Jan Boer

GATE POST LAYOUT

Hinge

On-center post spacing

Gate

Latch

A. *Trim the posts, and attach the cut stringers on top of the posts with 3" galvanized deck screws.*

TOOLS & MATERIALS

- Tools & materials for setting posts (page 24)
- Tape measure
- Chalk line
- Line level
- Reciprocating saw or handsaw
- Paintbrush
- Circular saw
- Hammer
- Drill
- Level
- Wood sealer/protectant or paint

- Pressure-treated, cedar, or redwood lumber:
  - 4 × 4s, 10 ft.
  - 2 × 4s, 8 ft.
  - 1 × 6s, 8 ft.
- Galvanized 2 × 4 fence brackets
- 4d galvanized nails
- 3" galvanized deck screws
- 6d galvanized nails
- 2" galvanized deck screws
- ⅛" piece of scrap wood
- Prefabricated gate & hardware
- Wood scraps for shims

Hold or tack the board against the posts, and scribe the back side along the edges of the posts.

4. Cut the stringers ¼" shorter than marked, so they will slide into the brackets easily. Coat the cut ends of the stringers with sealer and let them dry.

5. Nail the stringers into place, using 6d galvanized nails. If the stringers are angled to accommodate a slope, bend the bottom flanges of the brackets to match the angles of the stringers.

Step C: Attach the Siding

1. Beginning at an end post, measure from the ground to the top edge of the top stringer and add 8½". Cut a 1 × 6 to this length and seal its edges.

2. Position the 1 × 6 so that its top extends 10½" above the top stringer, leaving a 2" gap at the bottom. Make sure the siding board is plumb, then attach it to the post and rails with pairs of 2" galvanized deck screws.

3. Measure, cut, and attach the remaining siding to the stringers, using the same procedure. Leave a gap of at least ⅛" between boards, using pieces of scrap wood for spacers. If necessary, rip boards at the ends of the fence to make them fit.

Step D: Hang the Gate

1. Attach three hinges to the gate frame, evenly spaced and parallel to the gate edge.

2. Shim the gate into position between the gate posts. Drill pilot holes and attach the hinges to the gate post, using the screws provided with the hinge hardware.

3. On the opposite side, attach the latch hardware to the fence and to the gate.

4. Open and close the gate to make sure the latch works correctly. Make adjustments if necessary. Paint the fence or coat with sealer.

C. *Measure and cut the siding to size. Attach the siding to the framework, spacing them at least ⅛" apart.*

B. *Attach the fence brackets to the inside faces of the posts. Position the stringers in the brackets, then nail them in place.*

D. *Attach the hinges according to the manufacturer's directions, then hang the gate and install the latch hardware.*

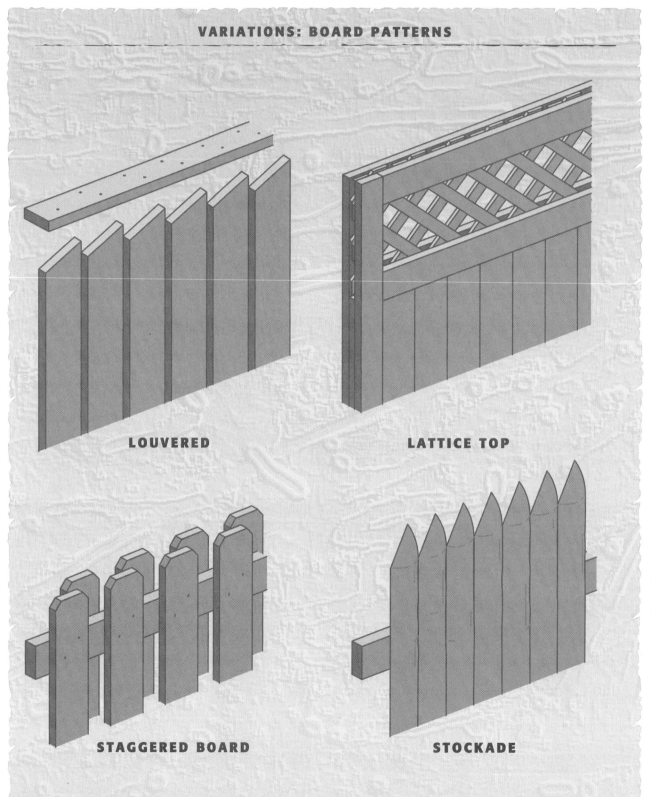

VARIATIONS: BOARD PATTERNS

LOUVERED

LATTICE TOP

STAGGERED BOARD

STOCKADE

Panel

Panel fences are one of the easiest, quickest types of fences you can build. They're also reasonably priced and ideal for yards that are flat or have a steady, gradual slope.

Preassembled fence panels come in a wide variety of popular styles. The one disadvantage is that not all panels are as well built as you might like. Shop around to find well-constructed panels made of high-quality materials. Be sure to choose and purchase your panels before setting

your posts, so you can space the posts accurately.

Although you can trim panels to fit between the posts if necessary, doing that can be difficult. Try to plan a layout that uses only full-sized panels.

If the fence line includes a slope, decide whether to contour or step the fence (pages 21 to 23) and plan accordingly.

TOOLS & MATERIALS

- Tools & materials for setting posts (page 24)
- Tape measure
- Mason's string
- Carpenter's level
- Line level
- Hammer
- Stepladder
- Reciprocating saw or handsaw
- Paintbrush

- Pressure-treated, cedar, or redwood 4 × 4 posts, 10 ft.
- Prefabricated fence panels
- Galvanized fence brackets
- 4d galvanized nails
- 1" galvanized deck screws
- Prefabricated gate & hardware
- Post caps
- Galvanized casing nails
- Wood sealer/protectant or paint
- Wood blocks

HOW TO BUILD A PANEL FENCE

Step A: Test-fit the Preassembled Panels

1. Lay out the fence line (pages 18 to 19) and in-stall posts (pages 24 to 25). Space the posts to fit the preassembled panels you've purchased. Let the concrete cure for at least 2 days.

2. Test-fit the panels, positioning each so the bottom of the panel will be 2" above ground level. Check the panel for plumb, using a level, then outline it on the inside faces of the posts.

3. On level sites, use a line level to ensure that the panels will be level. On a sloped site where panels

VARIATION: FENCE PANELS

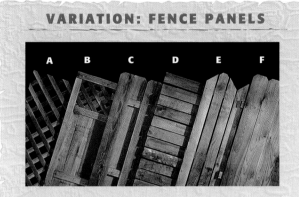

Preassembled fence panels are an attractive, timesaving option when building a fence. The entire panel is attached to the posts, eliminating the need to individually cut and attach stringers.

Some popular styles of prefabricated panels include:

A. Lattice panels	D. Horizontal board
B. Solid panels with lattice tops	E. Modified picket
C. Staggered board	F. Dog-eared board

will be installed step-fashion, try to maintain a uniform vertical drop with each panel.

Step B: Mark Panel Position & Attach Brackets

1. Align and attach a bracket against the bottom of the outline, using 4d galvanized nails.

A. *Lay out the fence line and set the posts. Test-fit a panel and outline its position on the inside faces of the posts.*

B. *Align the bottom of the first bracket 2" above ground level. Evenly space two more brackets inside the outline, attaching each bracket with 4d galvanized nail (inset).*

4. Attach two more, evenly spaced, brackets inside the outline. Bend the bottom flange of both these brackets flat against the post.

Step C: Attach Fence Panels

1. Working from above, slide the panel into the brackets until it rests on the bottom flange of the lowest bracket.

2. Attach the panels from each side by driving 1" galvanized deck screws through the holes in the brackets.

Step D: Attach the Gate Hardware & the Gate

1. Align three evenly spaced hinges on the gate frame so that the pins are straight and flush with the edge of the gate. Attach the hinges to the gate frame with the screws provided with the hardware.

2. Shim the gate into position between the gate posts, with the hinge pins resting against one post. Attach the hinges to the post, using the screws provided by the manufacturer.

4. Attach the latch hardware to the other gate post and then to the gate, using the screws provided by the manufacturer.

5. Open and close the gate to make sure the latch works correctly, and adjust if necessary.

Step E: Trim & Decorate Post Tops

1. Use a reciprocating saw or handsaw to trim the tops uniformly.

2. Cover flat post tops with decorative wood or metal caps, attaching the caps with galvanized casing nails. If you're not going to use post caps, trim the posts to a point to help them shed water.

3. Paint the fence or coat with wood sealer/protectant.

D. *Attach three evenly spaced hinges to the gate frame. Shim the gate in place and attach the hinges on the gate post. Attach the latch hardware to the gate and then to the opposite post.*

C. *Slide the fence panels into the brackets from above, until they rest on the bottom flanges of the lowest brackets.*

E. *Trim the post tops to size, using a reciprocating saw. Cover each post top with a decorative post cap, or trim it to a point to help shed water. Paint or coat the fence with sealer.*

Shadow Box

Garden tools and implements seem to multiply in the night. Many of today's tools are attractive as well as functional—rather than hiding them in a garage or shed, why not use them to accessorize a fence bay? To turn a fence bay into a shadow box:

Step A: Prepare the Materials & Install the Vertical Supports

1. Determine the number and location of the vertical supports. Measure the distance between the stringers in those locations, and cut 2 × 4s to length with a circular saw.

2. Determine the locations of the shelves and measure the distance between the vertical supports in those locations. Cut 1 × 4s to length.

3. Paint, stain, or seal the lumber to match or complement the fence. If you like the look shown here, paint the sections of the fence siding as well.

4. Position the vertical supports and secure them to the stringers with pairs of angle irons and 1" galvanized deck screws.

Step B: Prepare the Shelves

1. Measure the diameter of your pots, just below the edge of the rim. Use a compass to draw appropriately-sized, evenly-spaced circles across one of the shelves. Cut out the circles, using a jig saw.

2. Attach decorative molding to the front edge of one shelf, using exterior wood glue and galvanized finish nails.

3. Drill four evenly-spaced holes

A. *Secure the vertical supports with pairs of angle irons and 1" galvanized deck screws.*

TOOLS & MATERIALS

- Tape measure
- Circular saw
- Paintbrushes & roller
- Drill
- Compass
- Jig saw
- Hammer
- 1 × 4 lumber
- Paint, stain, or sealer
- 1" galvanized deck screws
- Angle irons, 4 for each support or shelf
- 2" galvanized deck screws
- Exterior wood glue
- Decorative molding
- Galvanized finish nails
- Decorative knobs or pegs (4)
- Clay pots
- Gardening tools
- Herbs, annuals, trailing vines

Existing section of fence — *Top stringer* — *Horizontal support for pegs* — *Pot shelf* — *1 × 4 shelf with decorative edge* — *Vertical support* — *Bottom stringer*

across a horizontal support, using a bit that matches the size of the stems on your knobs or pegs. Screw in the knobs or secure the pegs with exterior wood glue.

Step C: Install the Shelves

1. Install the horizontal supports, using 2" galvanized deck screws.

2. Position the shelves according to your planned layout, and secure them with pairs of angle irons and 1" galvanized deck screws.

Step D: Add Accessories

Add pots of herbs or annuals. Hang gardening tools from the pegs. If you want to get even more creative, you could install a brass hook on a vertical support to hold a gardening hat or apron.

It might also be fun to put a mirror behind the pot holder. Have a mirror cut to fit that section, seal the back with polyurethane, and fasten it with construction adhesive.

B. *Cut holes for pots in one 1 × 4, add decorative molding to another, and add knobs to a third.*

C. *Drive 2" galvanized deck screws through the face of the horizontal support and into the siding.*

D. *Add accessories and embellishments as desired.*

Framed Opening

Framing an opening into a broad expanse of solid fence can create a lively view or let you display a decorative piece. To frame an opening:

Step A: Mark the Opening

1. Measure the item to be framed into the fence or decide on the dimensions of the opening.

2. Select the location for the opening. Consider the direction of the sun if you're framing in a piece of stained glass or the view beyond the fence if you're planning a simple window.

3. Use a level and a framing square to mark the opening on the siding of the fence.

Step B: Cut an Opening in the Siding

Drill a hole in one corner of the opening, then slip the blade of a jig saw or reciprocating saw into that hole and cut along the marked lines.

Step C: Add the Frame

1. Measure the opening. To calculate the lengths for the top and bottom pieces of the frame, add 7" to the width of the opening. Mark and cut four pieces of 1 × 4 lumber to this length.

2. For the four side pieces, mark and cut 1 × 4 lumber to match the height of the opening exactly.

3. Paint, stain, or seal the frame pieces to match or complement the fence. Allow to dry thoroughly.

4. Carefully align the side pieces with the edge of the opening and clamp them in place. Drill evenly-spaced pilot holes, then drive 2¼" galvanized deck screws through the trim and siding and into the trim on the back side of the fence. Repeat this procedure with the top and bottom pieces.

Step D: Position the Display Piece & Add Trim

1. Measure the display piece and determine how it will sit within the opening. Cut 1 × 1s to fit around the piece, framing both the front and back.

2. On the back side of the opening, drill pilot holes and drive

finish nails through the 1 × 1s and into the frame pieces.

3. Position the display piece and add the trim on the front side. Carefully nail the trim in place, using finish nails and a tack hammer.

TOOLS & MATERIALS

- Tape measure
- Level
- Framing square
- Drill
- Jig saw or reciprocating saw
- Paintbrushes & roller

- Circular saw
- Spring clamps
- Hammer
- Tack hammer
- Display piece
- 1 × 4 lumber

- Paint, stain, or sealer
- 2¼" galvanized deck screws
- 1 × 1 lumber
- Finish nails

A. *Determine measurements and draw an opening on the siding of the fence, using a framing square and a level. Make certain the opening is square, plumb, and properly positioned.*

B. *Drill a pilot hole in one corner of the outline. Insert the blade of a jig saw and cut along the marked lines.*

C. *Sandwich the opening with 1 × 4 trim and clamp the trim in place. Drill pilot holes and drive 2¼" galvanized deck screws through the trim and siding.*

D. *Position the first set of trim pieces and secure them with finish nails. Position the display piece and the second set of trim. Carefully nail the trim in place, using a tack hammer and finish nails.*

Display Shelves

As interest in gardening continues to grow, so does the array of garden ornaments available from stores, catalogs, and E-tailers. This mirrored display shelf made from a salvaged window sash is a perfect place to show off treasured pieces.

HOW TO BUILD
DISPLAY SHELVES

Step A: Create a Frame

1. Select a window sash and measure each side. (If you're using a salvaged or antique window, the unit may not be square.)

2. Cut 1 × 6 lumber to match the top and bottom of the sash, using a circular saw. Subtract 1½" from the length of the sides of the sash and cut 1 × 6s to match.

3. Form the pieces into a frame for the window sash, lapping the joints as shown on page 43. Secure the joints with exterior wood glue and finish nails. NOTE: The wood in salvaged or antique windows may be fragile. Drill pilot holes for the nails, to avoid splitting the wood.

4. Prime and paint the frame to match the window sash. (We used a base coat, crackle medium, and a top coat to mimic the weathered surface of the window sash we had selected.)

Step B: Add the Back & Mirror

1. Measure the inside dimensions of the 1 × 6 frame and have a mirror cut to size.

2. Measure the outside dimensions of the 1 × 6 frame and cut a piece of ½" exterior plywood to size. Prime and paint the plywood, including the edges.

3. Set the plywood back on top of the frame, with the edges carefully aligned. Drill pilot holes approximately every 4", and secure the plywood to the frame, using 1½" galvanized deck screws.

4. Apply construction adhesive to the back of the mirror and carefully secure it to the plywood, inside the frame. Allow the construction adhesive to dry according to manufacturer's directions.

A. *Cut 1 × 6s to create a frame around the perimeter of the window. Form butt joints, and join them with exterior wood glue and finish nails.*

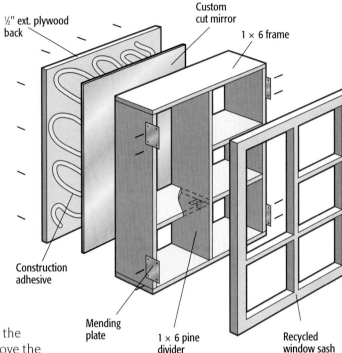

½" ext. plywood back

Custom cut mirror

1 × 6 frame

Construction adhesive

Mending plate

1 × 6 pine divider

Recycled window sash

TOOLS & MATERIALS

- Tape measure
- Circular or trim saw
- Hammer
- Drill
- Paintbrush
- Multi-paned window sash
- 1 × 6 lumber
- Exterior wood glue
- Exterior primer and paint to match window frame
- 4d finish nails
- Mirror, custom cut
- ½" exterior plywood
- 1½" galvanized deck screws
- Construction adhesive
- Caulk gun
- Angle irons, 4 for each shelf
- ½" wood screws
- 4 flat mending plates

Step C: Install the Shelves

1. Cut a 1 × 6 divider to fit between the top and bottom of the frame as well as a 1 × 6 shelf for every horizontal muntin. Prime and paint the brace and shelves to match the window sash. Allow to dry.

2. Set the window sash over the frame, then position the vertical divider and horizontal shelves so they align with the muntins. Mark the frame to show the location of the divider and the shelves, then remove the sash and attach the divider and shelves with angle irons.

Step D: Connect the Window & Frame

1. Attach a pair of 3 × 2" flat mending plates to the side of the window sash—one 2" from the bottom of the sash and one 2" from the top. Align the window sash on top of the frame and attach the plates to the frame as well. Repeat on the opposite side.

B. *Cut ½" exterior plywood to fit the frame. Screw it in place, then attach a custom-cut mirror to the inside, using construction adhesive.*

C. *Cut shelves to fit; prime and paint. Attach shelves with pairs of angle irons and ½" wood screws.*

D. *Secure the window to the frame, using 3 × 2" flat mending plates and ½" wood screws.*

Picket

For generations, the stereotypical dream home has been a vine-covered cottage surrounded by a white picket fence. But these days, the diversity in designs and styles of this classic American fence make it adaptable to any home, from a three-story Victorian to a modest rambler.

The charm of a picket fence lies in its open and inviting appearance. The repetitive structure and spacing create a pleasing rhythm that welcomes family and friends while maintaining a fixed property division.

Traditionally, picket fences are 36 to 48" tall. Our version is 48" tall, the posts are spaced 96" on center, and the pickets are spaced 1¾" apart. It's important that the spacing appear to be consistent. Using a jig simplifies that process, and, if necessary, you can spread any incongruity across many pickets to mask the discrepancy.

Picket fences are traditionally white; however, matching your house's trim color or stain can be an eye-catching alternative. You'll need to apply two coats of paint or stain. If you prime and paint all the materials before construction, apply the second coat after the fence is completed to cover any marks, smudges, and nail or screw heads.

There are a number of picket styles to choose from. Most building centers carry a variety, or you can design your own by simply creating a template. If you need a large quantity of pickets or want to use an intricate design, contact a cabinet shop in your area—the time saved may be worth the added expense.

© Charles Mann

TOOLS & MATERIALS

- Tools & materials for setting posts (page 24)
- Circular saw
- Jig saw
- Paintbrush and roller
- Tape measure
- Reciprocating saw or handsaw
- Spring clamps
- Framing square
- Drill

- Pressure-treated, cedar, or redwood lumber:
  - 1 × 4s, 8 ft. (9 per bay)
  - 2 × 4s, 8 ft. (2 per bay)
  - 4 × 4s, 8 ft. (2 per bay)
- Paint, stain, or sealer
- 16d galvanized nails
- 1½" galvanized deck screws
- Fence post finials

HOW TO BUILD A PICKET FENCE

Step A: Prepare the Materials

1. Lay out the fence line with stakes and mason's string (pages 18 to 19). Space the post locations every 96" on center.

2. Count the 4 × 4 posts and estimate the number of pickets you'll need to complete the project. Since it's likely you'll make a cutting error or two, estimate enough lumber to compensate.

3. If you're creating your own pickets, cut 1 × 4s to length. (Our design calls for 46" pickets.) Cut simple pointed-pickets with a circular saw. For more elaborate designs like the one shown here, make a template, then use a jig saw to cut the pickets.

4. Apply the first coat of paint, stain, or sealer.

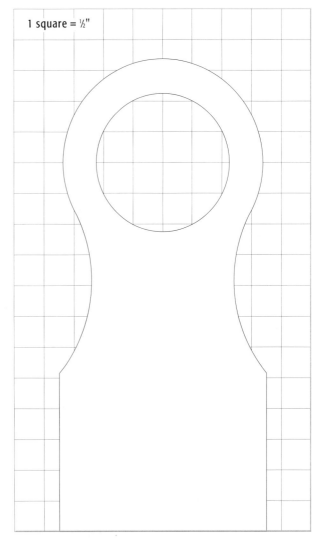

1 square = ½"

A. *Mark the fence line and calculate the number of posts and pickets required. Cut pickets, using a template and a jig saw.*

Cutting List

Each 96" bay requires:

Part	Type	Size	Number
Posts	4 × 4	78"	2
Pickets	1 × 4	46"	18
Stringers	2 × 4	92½"	2
Jig	1 × 4	1¾" × 46"	1

Step B: Set the Posts

1. Set the posts (pages 24 to 25). Allow the concrete footings to cure for 2 days.

2. Measure up 48" from the base of each post and mark cutting lines.

3. Trim the posts along the cutting lines, using a reciprocating saw or handsaw.

Step C: Build the Framework

1. On each post, measure and mark a line 6" down from the top of the post to indicate the upper stringer position, and 36½" from the top to indicate the lower stringer.

B. *Set the posts, then mark cutoff lines and trim them to 48" above ground level.*

2. At the upper stringer marks on the first two posts, clamp an 8 ft. 2 × 4 with the top edge of the 2 × 4 flush with the mark. Scribe the post outline on the back of the stringer at each end. Remove and cut the upper stringer to size, using a circular saw.

3. Position the upper stringer between the two posts, set back ¾" from the face of the posts. Toenail the stringer into place with 16d galvanized nails.

4. Repeat #2 and #3 to install the remaining stringers, both upper and lower.

Step D: Space & Hang the Pickets

1. To compensate for slope or shorter sections, calculate the picket spacing: Decide on the number of pickets you want between posts. Multiply that number by the width of a single picket. This is the total width of pickets between the posts. Subtract that number from the total distance between the posts. The remainder equals the unoccupied space. Divide that number by the number of pickets minus 1 (the number of spaces that will exist between the posts). The resulting number equals the picket spacing.

Picket Spacing Example:

18 (pickets) × 3½" (picket width) = 63" (total picket width).
92½" (space between posts) − 63" = 29½" (unoccupied space).
29½" ÷ 17 (18 pickets − 1) = 1¾" (space between pickets).

NOTE: Not all calculations will work out evenly. If your figures come out uneven, make slight adjustments across the entire fence section.

C. *Mark the stringer position on the posts, then scribe and cut the stringer to size. Toenail the stringer in place (inset).*

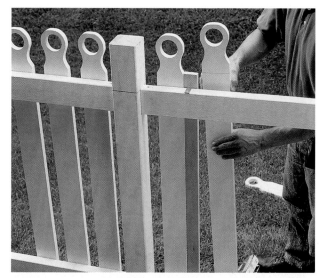

D. *Calculate the picket spacing and make a spacing jig. Position the first picket and secure it with 1½" galvanized deck screws. Using the spacing jig, position and install the remaining pickets.*

2. To make a spacing jig, rip a 1 × 4 to the spacing size—1¾" in this project. Attach a scrap of wood to one end of the board as a cleat.

3. Draw a reference mark on each picket, 6" down from the peak.

4. Place a picket flat against the stringers and slide it flush against the post. Adjust the picket until the reference line is flush with the top edge of the upper stringer. Drill pilot holes and attach the picket, using 1½" deck screws.

5. Hang the jig on the upper stringer and hold it flush against the attached picket. Position a new picket flush against the jig and attach it. Reposition the jig and continue along the fence line.

Step E: Apply Finishing Details

1. Attach fence post finials for detail. Use a straightedge to draw lines from corner to corner on the top of the post to determine the center. Drill a pilot hole where the lines intersect and screw a finial into the center of each post.

2. For painted fences, apply the second coat.

E. *Determine the center of the post tops, drill pilot holes, and screw in fence post finials.*

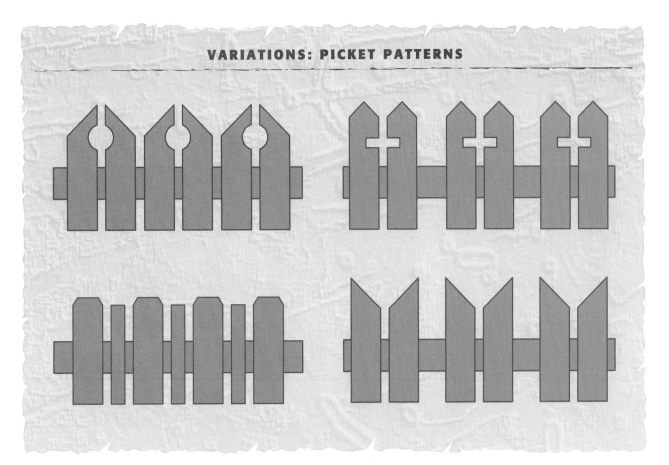

VARIATIONS: PICKET PATTERNS

Post & Rail

Post and rail construction can be used to build fences in a surprising range of styles, from a rustic split rail fence to the more genteel post & rail fence, with or without a capped top.

Because they use so little lumber, split rail fences are an inexpensive way to cover a large area of land. We show you how to build this fence by setting the posts in gravel-and-dirt footings. This method is common in some regions, but isn't appropriate everywhere. You can set the posts in concrete (pages 24 to 25) if required by the building codes in your area.

One other note: if you don't want to cut mortises, most lumberyards offer pre-mortised posts and tapered stringers that can be used to build split rail fences.

Post and rail fences, which typically are painted but sometimes stained and sealed, require more lumber and more upkeep than split rail fences, but in certain settings nothing else will do. There are endless variations on rail placement, but the directions shown on pages 50 and 51 will give you a good understanding of the basics involved. You should be able to adapt the plans and build just about any design that appeals to you.

HOW TO BUILD A SPLIT RAIL FENCE

Step A: Prepare the Posts

1. Plot the fence line (page 18), spacing posts every 72" on center. Dig the postholes (page 24).

2. From the top of each post, measure and mark points 6" and

26½" down the center. Outline 2"-wide by 4"-tall mortises at each mark, using a cardboard template.

Step B: Cut the Mortises

1. Drill a series of 1" holes inside each mortise outline, drilling through the backside if necessary. Drill only halfway through for end posts, and halfway through on adjacent sides for corner posts.

2. Remove the remaining wood from the mortises with a hammer

TOOLS & MATERIALS

- Tools & materials for plotting a fence line (page 18)
- Cardboard
- Chalk line
- Shovel
- Combination square
- Drill, with 1"-bit
- 2" wood chisel
- Chisel & hammer
- Reciprocating saw with a 6" wood blade
- Rubber mallet
- Refer to cutting list for lumber
- Coarse gravel

Cutting List

Each 72" bay requires:

Part	Type	Size	Number
Posts	4 × 4	66"	2
Stringers	4 × 4	72"	2

Top stringer

6"

Mortis

26½"

Bottom stringer

Tenon

2 tenons fit into mortis

and chisel.

Step C: Shape the Tenons

1. Snap a straight chalk line down the sides of the stringers.

2. On one end, draw a straight line from the chalk line mark at the edge, to the center of the timber, using a combination square.

3. At the center, draw a 1½"-long line perpendicular to the first, extending ¾" from each side. From each end of this line, draw perpendicular lines up to the edge of the timber. You will have outlined a rough, 1½" × 1½"-square tenon end.

4. Measure and mark 3½" down from the end stringer for the tenon length.

5. Rough cut the tenons, using a reciprocating saw with a 6" wood blade. If necessary, shape the tenons with a hammer and chisel to fit the mortises.

Step D: Set the Posts & Attach the Stringers

1. Fill the postholes with 6" of gravel, and insert the first post. Because each post is cut to size, make sure the post top measures 36" from the ground. If it sits too high, lay a board over the post top and tap down with a rubber mallet. If it's too low, add more gravel. Leave 6" of clearance between the position of the bottom stringer and the ground.

2. Begin to fill the posthole with gravel and dirt. Every few inches, tamp the dirt around the post with the end of your shovel, and

check the post for plumb.

3. Place the next post in the posthole without setting it. Insert the tenons of the stringers into the mortises of the set, first post. Insert the other ends of the stringers to the unset post. Adjust the post to fit the stringers if necessary.

4. Plumb the post and set with a dirt and gravel footing. Repeat this procedure of setting a post, then attaching the stringers. Alternate the stringers so the tenons of one stringer face up and the tenons of the next stringer face down, creating a tight fit in the mortise. Plumb each post as you go.

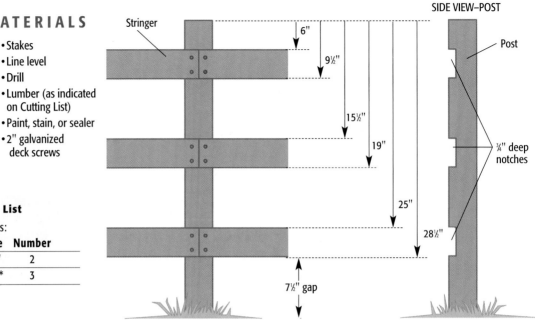

SIDE VIEW–POST

Stringer

6"

9½"

15½"

19"

25"

28½"

7½" gap

Post

¾" deep notches

TOOLS & MATERIALS

- Tools & materials for setting posts (page 24)
- Tape measure
- Bar clamps
- Circular saw
- Framing square
- Chisel & hammer
- Paintbrush & roller

- Stakes
- Line level
- Drill
- Lumber (as indicated on Cutting List)
- Paint, stain, or sealer
- 2" galvanized deck screws

Cutting List

Each 72" bay requires:

Part	Type	Size	Number
Posts	4 × 4	66"	2
Stringers	1 × 4	72"*	3

*add 1¼" for end stringers

HOW TO BUILD A POST & RAIL FENCE

Step A: Prepare the Posts

1. Mark the fence line (pages 18 to 19). Mark and dig postholes 72" on center (pages 24 to 25).

2. Cut 4 × 4 posts to 66". Measure and mark at 6", 9½", 15½", 19", 25", and 28½" down from the top of two posts.

3. Gang several posts between the marked posts and clamp them together, using bar clamps. Use a framing square to extend the marks across all the posts. Mark the notches with an "X" between each pair of marks.

Step B: Notch the Posts

1. Make a series of cuts inside

each set of reference lines, using a circular saw with the blade depth set at ¾".

2. Remove the remaining wood in each notch, using a hammer and chisel. Remove wood only to the depth of the original cuts so the stringers will sit flush with the face of the post.

Step C: Set the Posts & Attach the Stringers

1. Cut the stringers (see cutting list above). Paint, stain, or seal all the lumber and allow it to dry.

2. Brace the posts into position (pages 24 to 25) with the notches facing out. Run a mason's string and set a level line; keep the notches aligned and the tops of the posts 36" above the ground. If

a post is too high, lay a board over it and tap down, using a rubber mallet. If it's too low, add gravel beneath it. Be sure there is 7½" between the bottom of the lowest notch and the ground. Set the posts in concrete and let it cure for 2 days.

3. Fit a 73½" stringer into the notches in the first pair of posts. Position it to cover the entire notch in the first post and half of the notch in the second. Attach the stringer, using 2" galvanized deck screws. Install the other two stringers to this pair of posts.

4. Butt a stringer against the first one and attach it securely. Repeat with remaining stringers.

TOOLS & MATERIALS

- Tools & materials for setting posts (page 24)
- Tape measure
- Reciprocating saw or handsaw
- Combination square
- Circular saw
- Drill

- Refer to cutting list for lumber
- 2" galvanized deck screws
- 3" galvanized deck screws
- Paint, stain, or sealer

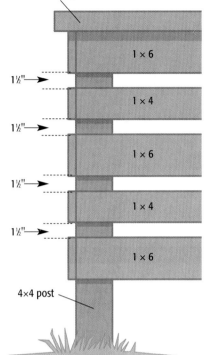

2 × 6 Cap

1 × 6

1½"→

1 × 4

1½"→

1 × 6

1½"→

1 × 4

1½"→

1 × 6

4×4 post

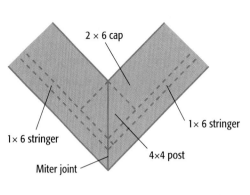

2 × 6 cap

1 × 6 stringer

1× 6 stringer

4×4 post

Miter joint

TOP VIEW–DETAIL

HOW TO BUILD A CAPPED POST & RAIL FENCE

Step A: Set the Posts

1. Mark the fence line (pages 18 to 19), spacing posts 72" on center.

2. Cut the lumber as indicated on the cutting list at right. Paint, stain, or seal the posts and let them dry.

2. Dig postholes and set the posts (pages 24 to 25). Let the footings cure for 2 days.

3. Measure and mark each post at 36" from the ground. Trim with a reciprocating saw or handsaw. Touch up the finish on top of the posts.

Cutting List

Each 72" bay requires:

Part	Type	Size	Number
Posts	4 × 4	66"	2
Stringers	1 × 4	72"*	2
	1 × 6	72"*	3
Top cap	2 × 6	72"*	1

*add 1¾" end post stringers and top cap

4. Mark a line down the center of the outside face of each post (except the end or gate posts).

Step B: Attach the Stringers

1. Measure from the reference line on one post to the line on the next. For each bay, cut two 1 × 4s and three 1 × 6s to this length. For the last bay, measure from the last reference line to the outside edge of the end post. Paint, stain, or seal the stringers.

2. Position a 1 × 6 against the faces of two posts with its top edge flush with the top of the posts and its ends flush with the reference lines. Clamp the stringer in place, then attach it on both ends, using pairs of 2" galvanized deck screws.

3. On each post, mark a line 1½" from the bottom of the 1 × 6. Position and attach a 1 × 4 as described above.

4. Alternate 1 × 6s and 1 × 4s,

spacing them 1½" apart.

Step C: Attach the Cap Stringer

1. Measure and cut 2 × 6s to fit between post tops. Add 1¾" on the end posts so the cap stringers extend beyond the posts. For corners, cut the ends at 45° angles, using a circular saw.

2. Position a cap stringer on the post tops, flush with the back of the posts and extending 1¼" beyond the front. Make sure the ends are centered on the posts, and attach the caps, using 3" galvanized deck screws.

Vinyl

Made of polyvinyl chloride (PVC), the same durable material as vinyl house siding, vinyl fencing is virtually maintenance-free. It will never rust, rot, peel, splinter, or crack. The material itself never needs painting and is UV resistant, so it's unlikely to fade.

Most vinyl fence products are installed in the same general way, but there are some differences between details. It's important to read and follow the manufacturer's instructions precisely. Many manufacturers also provide toll-free numbers where you can get additional advice and help, if necessary.

Vinyl fence materials are pre-cut to length and shipped in unassembled kits. The pre-routed holes in the posts make it easy to insert and lock the pieces together.

It's essential to reinforce each corner, end, and gate post with concrete and rebar. If the fence is 60" or higher, it's a good idea to reinforce each of the posts. If concrete were allowed to seep into the stringers, it would cause them to sag over time. To prevent that problem, tape or plug the ends of each stringer before installing it.

Since most vinyl fencing is ordered directly from the manufacturer or through a distributor, you'll have an opportunity to ask and answer questions before you place an order. Lay out your fence line and consider any special challenges, such as slope issues. With that information in hand, a sales representative may be able to help you customize the materials and simplify the installation process.

TOOLS & MATERIALS

- Tools & materials for setting posts (page 24)
- Cordless drill or screwdriver
- Level
- PVC vinyl fencing materials
- Duct tape
- #3 rebar
- Rebar separator clips
- Construction adhesive

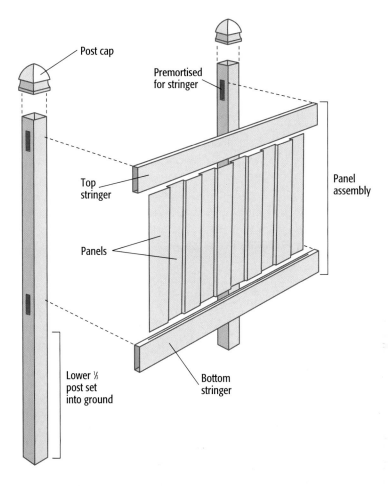

Post cap

Premortised for stringer

Top stringer

Panels

Panel assembly

Lower ⅓ post set into ground

Bottom stringer

HOW TO INSTALL VINYL FENCING

NOTE: These are general installation tips. Refer to the manufacturer's instructions for your specific fence style.

Step A: Prepare the Materials

1. Mark the fence line (pages 18 to 19), spacing the post hole locations according to the manufacturer's recommendations.

2. Sort and check the materials to be sure you have received all the proper fence pieces and hardware.

3. Cover both ends of each stringer with duct tape. Make sure there are no gaps or holes that would allow concrete to seep into the stringer later when you fill the posts.

Step B: Assemble the Panels

1. Insert the panel pieces into the pre-routed holes of the bottom stringer. Make sure each piece fits securely. If not, add duct tape to the bottom of the pieces so the fit is tighter.

2. Attach the top stringer to the panels. Work from one end and adjust the panel pieces to fit into the pre-routed holes. Make sure the stringer fits tightly around the panel pieces.

3. Secure the stringer to the panels with the self-tapping screws provided by the manufacturer.

Step C: Set the First Post

1. Position the first post. Because the posts are manufactured to size, the posts must sit precisely at the height of the fence. If a post is too high, lay a board over the top and gently tap it down, using a rubber mallet. If it's too low, add gravel beneath it. Be sure to leave enough room for a 2" gap between the bottom of the fence and the ground.

3. Mix concrete in a wheelbarrow or mixing trough, and set the post (pages 24 to 25). Use a level to make sure the post is plumb on adjacent sides. Brace the plumbed post into position with stakes and scrap pieces of 2 × 4 tied or taped to the post. Let the concrete cure.

A. *Place tape over the ends of the lower stringers so concrete cannot seep into them from the posts.*

Step D: Attach the Panels

1. Set the next post and pour the concrete footing, but do not brace the post just yet.

2. With the assistance of another person, fit the panel between the posts. Insert the top and bottom stringers to the pre-routed holes of the first (previous set) post.

3. Insert the stringers on the other end of the panel into the next post. If necessary, adjust the post to accommodate the stringers.

4. Inside of the post, drive a screw (provided with the kit) through the top stringer to secure it.

5. Plumb the post and brace it with 2 × 4s. Repeat this procedure of setting a post, then attaching a panel. Plumb each post and brace it securely in place before you begin work on the next panel.

Step E: Reinforce the End and Corner Posts

1. If you're installing a gate, mount the hinge and latch hardware to the gate posts.

2. Connect two 72"-lengths of #3 rebar with rebar-separator clips for every end and corner post. Place one clip 6" down from the top of each piece and another 12" up from the bottom.

3. Position the rebar assembly inside the post, with the pieces of rebar siting in opposing corners.

4. Fill the post with concrete until the rebar is covered, leaving at least 6" of clearance at the top. Wipe off any excess or seepage.

Step F: Attach the Finishing Details

1. Attach post caps with glue or screws, if provided by the manufacturer. If you use glue, apply it to the inside edge of the cap, and then attach the cap to the post top. Wipe off any excess glue as soon as possible.

2. Cover exposed screw heads with screw caps, if provided.

3. Wash the fence with a mild detergent and water.

NOTE: PVC vinyl can be permanently discolored by some wasp or insect sprays. Use these products with caution around vinyl fences as well as vinyl siding.

B. *Attach the panels by working from one end and adjusting them to fit the pre-routed holes of the bottom stringer.*

C. *Keep the posts plumb with 2 × 4 braces attached to stakes driven into the ground. Duct tape is strong enough to hold the braces to the vinyl posts without causing any damage.*

Shown cut away for clarity

D. *Drive a screw through the top stringer inside of the post. The screw should be tight against the inside wall of the post.*

Shown cut away for clarity

E. *Attach the rebar separator clips and set the rebar into position in the posts. Fill the post with concrete to within 6" of the top of the post.*

F. *Attach each post cap, using glue or screws, if provided by the manufacturer.*

VARIATIONS:

Louvered fences filter sightlines, providing privacy without completely obscuring the view. Louvered fences are perfect for extremely windy climates—their variated structure diffuses wind effectively.

Photo courtesy of CertainTeed EverNew

Ornamental Metal

Post cap

Pre-routed holes

Post

Assembled fence section

Footing

Today's ornamental metal fences are designed to replicate the elegant wrought-iron designs of the past. They are made of aluminum and galvanized steel, with a powder-coat finish to help prevent rust. Styles range from the simple to the ornate, and are available in a variety of colors and sizes. These fences have become recent favorites for swimming pool enclosures.

Few home centers stock these materials, but some may be able to order them for you. Many manufacturers and distributors maintain web sites where you can get more information or place orders. A quick search of the internet should yield plenty of options.

As with any prefabricated fence, always read the manufacturer's instructions thoroughly before beginning installation. Installing these fences is generally simple, but does require two people.

The fence sections are manufactured or welded together in 48"- to 96"-long sections, and the posts are pre-cut. In our design, the posts have pre-routed holes for the stringer ends. Other designs use systems of brackets or fasteners.

If a fence section is too long, cut it to fit, using a hacksaw. Make sure to cut off only as much as necessary—it's vital to maintain a tight fit and proper spacing.

When slope is an issue, metal fencing can be contoured with the ground if the grade's rise is less then 12" over a 72" run. Anything greater will require stepping the fence (pages 21 to 23). If you're using brackets, simply determine the step measurement and set the brackets accordingly. Any routed holes in the posts will have to be cut on site.

TOOLS & MATERIALS

- Tools & materials for setting posts (page 24)
- Tape measure
- Rubber mallet
- Hacksaw
- Drill
- Ornamental metal fencing materials
- 1" self-tapping screws
- 2 × 4 scraps
- Mason's string
- Stakes

HOW TO INSTALL AN ORNAMENTAL METAL FENCE

NOTE: These are general installation tips. Refer to the manufacturer's instructions for your specific fence.

Step A: Set the First Post

1. Lay out and check the materials to be sure you have all the parts and hardware.

2. Mark the fence line with stakes and mason's string (pages 18 to 19). Space and dig the postholes according to local codes and the manufacturer's recommendations.

A. *Dig post holes and set the first post in concrete. Brace it with 2 × 4s on adjacent sides.*

3. Starting with a gate or end post, set the first post in place. Use a level to make sure the post is plumb on adjacent sides. Brace it with stakes and scrap pieces of 2 × 4 tied or taped to the post.

Because the posts are manufactured to size, the top of the post must be at fence height when it's set. Measure the height; if the post is too high, lay a board over it and gently tap it down, using a rubber mallet. If it's too low, add gravel beneath it.

4. Set the post in concrete (pages 24 to 25). Let the concrete cure—you'll use this post as a starting point for the remaining sections of the fence.

Step B: Attach the Panels

1. Set the next post in concrete, but don't brace it yet.

2. With the assistance of another person, insert the top and bottom stringers of a fence section to the pre-routed holes of the fixed end or gate post.

3. At the other end of the section, insert the stringer ends to the line post. If necessary, adjust the line post to accommodate the stringers.

4. For the corners, attach the first section, then trim the stringer ends of the adjacent section approximately 1", using a hacksaw, so the sections remain properly spaced.

Step C: Finish the Installation

1. Drive 1" self-tapping screws through the posts and into each stringer end to secure the fence sections to the posts.

2. Plumb the line post and brace it firmly, using 2 × 4s on adjacent sides.

B. *Insert the stringer ends of the fence section into the routed holes of the posts.*

3. Continue setting posts and attaching sections of fence, plumbing each post as you go. Let the concrete cure for at least 24 hours.

4. Attach finials to the posts, using a rubber mallet or set screws, if provided.

C. *Secure the stringers to the posts with 1" self-tapping screws.*

Chain Link

If you're looking for a strong, durable, and economical way to keep pets and children in—or out—of your yard, a chain link fence may be the perfect solution. Chain link fences require minimal maintenance and provide excellent security. And for yards that include slopes, it's a natural choice—the mesh flexes enough that it can be adjusted to follow the contours of most yards.

A 48"-tall fence—the most common choice for residential use—is what we've demonstrated here. The posts, fittings, and chain link mesh, which are made from galvanized metal, can be purchased at home centers and fencing retailers. The end, corner, and gate posts, called *terminal posts*, bear the stress of the entire fence line.

They're larger in diameter than line posts and require larger concrete footings. A footing three times the post diameter is sufficient for terminal posts.

The fittings are designed to accommodate slight alignment and height differences between terminal posts and line posts. *Tension bands*, which hold the mesh to the terminal posts, have one flat side to keep the mesh flush along the outside of the fence line. The *stringer ends* hold the top stringer in place and keep it aligned. *Loop caps* on the line posts position the top stringer to brace the mesh.

When the framework is in place, the mesh must be tightened against it. This is done a section at a time with a winch tool called a *come-along*. As you tighten the come-along, the tension is distributed evenly across the entire length of the mesh, stretching it taut against the framework. One note of caution: It's surprisingly easy to topple the posts if you over-tighten the come-along. To avoid this problem, tighten just until the links of the mesh are difficult to to squeeze together by hand.

For added stability, you can weave a heavy gauge wire through the mesh, approximately 4" above the ground. Pull the wire taut, and secure it to brace bands placed on the terminal posts.

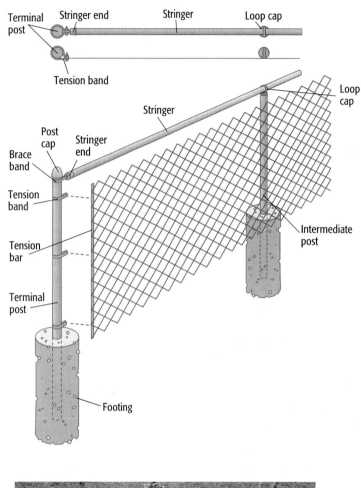

TOP VIEW

TOOLS & MATERIALS

- Tools & materials for setting posts (page 24)
- Tape measure
- Mason's string
- Stakes
- Chalk
- Wrench & pliers
- Hacksaw or pipe cutter
- Come-along (fence stretcher)

- Duct tape
- Galvanized terminal and line posts
- Galvanized fittings (see diagram)
- Bolts & nuts for chain link fence assembly
- Galvanized chain link mesh

HOW TO INSTALL A CHAIN LINK FENCE

Step A: Set the Posts

1. Mark the fence location with stakes and mason's string (pages 18 to 19). Measure and mark the post locations with stakes, every 96" on center.

2. Dig the postholes. For terminal posts (end, corner, and gate posts), dig the postholes 8" wide; for line posts, 6" wide.

3. Set the terminal posts in concrete (pages 24 to 25). Each terminal post should be 50" above the ground, or 2" above the fence height. Plumb each post, and brace it on adjacent sides with stakes and scrap pieces of 2 × 4 taped securely to the post.

4. From the top of each terminal post, measure down 4" and mark with chalk. Run a mason's string between the posts at the reference marks.

5. Fill the line post holes with concrete. Keep the post tops level with the mason's string, or 46" above the ground. Plumb each post and brace it on adjacent sides. Let the concrete cure for a day or two.

Step B: Attach the Fittings

1. Place three tension bands on every gate and end post. Place the first band 8" from the top, the second 24" from the top, and the third 8" off the ground. Make sure the flat side of each tension band faces the outside of the fence and points into the fence bay.

2. For corner posts, use six tension bands—two bands at each location. Point the flat sides of the bands in opposite directions.

3. Place a brace band approximately 3" below the top of each terminal post. Connect a stringer end to the brace band with a bolt and nut. The angled connection side of the stringer end should angle downward. Make sure the head of the bolt faces the outside of the proposed fence line.

4. For corners, place two brace bands on top of one

A. *Set the posts and brace them into position so they are plumb.*

B. *For a corner, place two brace bands 3" from the top of the post. Attach stringer ends with the angle side up to the upper brace band, and the angle side down to the lower band.*

C. *Cut the last piece of top stringer in a section to size. Adjust the brace band and stringer end to fit it in place.*

another. Connect a stringer end to the upper brace band so the angled connection side points upward, and one to the lower brace band so the angled connection side points downward.

5. Top each terminal post with a post cap and each line post with a loop cap. Make sure the loop cap openings are perpendicular to the proposed fence line, with the offset side facing the outside of the fence line.

Step C: Attach the Top Stringer

1. Start at one section, between two terminal posts, and feed the non-tapered end of a top stringer piece through the loop caps, toward a terminal post. Insert the non-tapered end into the cup of the stringer end. Make sure the stringer is snug. If necessary, loosen the brace band bolt and adjust it.

2. Continue to feed pieces of top stringer through the loop caps, fitting the non-tapered ends over the tapered ends. Use a sleeve to join two non-tapered ends, if necessary.

3. To fit the last piece of top stringer in the section, measure from where the taper begins on the previous piece to the inside back wall of the stringer end cup. Cut a piece of top stringer to size, using a hacksaw or pipe cutter. Connect the non-tapered end to the tapered end of the previous stringer. Loosen the brace band bolt and insert the cut end to the stringer

end assembly. Make sure the fittings remain snug.

4. Repeat for each section of the fence.

Step D: Apply the Chain Link Mesh

1. Unroll chain link mesh on the ground and stretch it along the fence line, from terminal post to terminal post.

2. Weave a tension bar through the end row of the mesh. Secure the tension bar to the tension bands on the terminal post with bolts and nuts. Make sure the bolt heads face the outside of the fence.

3. Pull the mesh taut along the fence line by hand, moving towards the terminal post at the other end. Set the mesh on end and lean it against the posts as you go.

Step E: Stretch the Chain Link Mesh

1. Weave the spread bar for a come-along through the mesh, approximately 48" from the final terminal post. Hook the spread bar of the come-along to the tension bar. Attach the other end of the come-along to the terminal post, roughly in the middle.

2. Tighten the come-along slowly, until the mesh is taut. Make sure to keep the top of the mesh lined up, so that the peaks of the links rise about 1" above the top stringer.

3. Pull the remaining chain link mesh tight to the terminal post by hand, and insert a tension bar where the mesh meets the tension braces.

D. *Weave a tension bar through the chain link mesh and attach it to the tension braces with bolts.*

Come-along

E. *Use a come-along to stretch the mesh taut against the fence. The mesh is tight enough when the links are difficult to squeeze together by hand.*

4. Remove any excess mesh by bending back both knuckle ends of one zig-zag strand in the mesh. Spin the strand counter-clockwise so it winds out of the links, separating the mesh into two.

5. Secure the tension bar to the tension bands with bolts and nuts, with the bolt heads facing the outside of the fence.

6. Use tie wire spaced every 12" to attach the mesh to the top stringer and line posts.

7. Repeat #1 through #6 for each section.

TIP: WEAVING CHAIN LINK MESH TOGETHER

If a section of chain link mesh comes up short between the terminal posts, you can add another piece by weaving two sections together.

With the first section laid out along the fence line, estimate how much more mesh is needed to reach the next terminal post. Over-estimate 6" or so, so you don't come up short again.

Detach the amount of mesh needed from the new roll by bending back the knuckle ends of one zig-zag strand in the mesh. Make sure the knuckles of the same strand are undone at the top and bottom of the fence. Spin the strand counter-clockwise to wind it out of the links, separating the mesh into two.

Place this new section of chain link at the short end of the mesh so the zig-zag patterns of the links line up with one another.

Weave the new section of chain link into the other section by reversing the unwinding process. Hook the end of the strand into the first link of the first section. Spin the strand clockwise until it winds into the first link of the second section, and so on. When the strand has connected the two sections, bend both ends back into a knuckle. Now you can attach the chain link mesh to the fence framework.

Brick & Cedar

This elegant fence is not nearly as difficult to construct as it looks. It does, however, require some time and effort, and will make use of both your carpentry and masonry skills. There are also quite a few necessary materials, which does increase the expense. But when the project is complete, you'll have an attractive, durable structure that will be the envy of the neighborhood.

The 72" brick pillars replace the posts of most fences. The footings need to be 4" longer and wider than the pillar on each side, 16 × 20" for this project.

To maintain an even ⅜" mortar joint spacing between bricks, create a story pole using a 2 × 2 marked with the spacing. After every few courses, hold the pole against the pillar to check the joints for a consistent thickness. Also make sure the pillars remain as plumb, level, and square as possible. Poor pillar construction greatly reduces strength and longevity of the pillars.

Attaching the stringers to the pillars is much easier than you may imagine.

Fence brackets and concrete screws are available that have as much holding power as lag bolts and anchors. Although other brands are available, we used ¼"-dia. TapCon concrete screws. The screws come with a special drill bit to make sure the embedment holes are the right diameter and depth, which simplifies the process for you.

The part of this project that looks the trickiest is creating the arched top of the cedar-slat fence sections. It can be achieved relatively easily by using a piece of PVC pipe. With the ends anchored, the pipe is flexible enough to bend into position and rigid enough to hold the form of the arch so it can be traced.

HOW TO BUILD A BRICK & CEDAR FENCE
Step A: Install the Footings

1. Measure and mark the fence line with stakes and mason's string (pages 18 to 19).

2. Determine the center of each pillar location along the fence line. To space the pillars at 96" edge to edge, drop a plumb bob 12" in from the end of the fence line, and then every 116". Place a stake at each pillar location.

TOOLS & MATERIALS

- Tools & materials for pouring footings
- Tape measure
- Level
- Plumb bob
- Wheelbarrow or mixing box
- Mason's trowel
- Jointing tool
- Aviation snips
- Drill
- Circular saw
- Hammer
- Jig saw
- Standard modular bricks (4 × 2⅔ × 8", 130 per pillar)
- 2 × 2 lumber, 10 ft.
- Chalk

- Type N mortar mix
- ¼" wooden dowel & vegetable oil
- ¼" wire mesh
- Capstone or concrete cap
- ⅜"-thick wood scraps
- 2 × 6 fence brackets (6 per bay)
- 1¼" countersink concrete screws
- Concrete drill bit
- Pressure-treated, cedar, or redwood lumber:
    1 × 6, 8 ft. (16 per bay)
    2 × 6, 8 ft. (3 per bay)
- 1½" galvanized deck screws
- 1½" finish nails (3)
- 96"-length of flexible ¼" PVC pipe

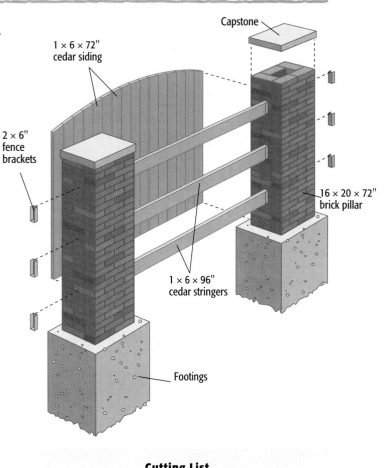

3. Outline 16 × 20" pillar footings at each location, then dig the trenches and pour the footings (pages 94 to 95). Let the footings cure for two days.

Step B: Lay the First Course

1. On a flat work surface, lay out a row of bricks, spaced ⅜" apart. Mark the identical spacing on a 2 × 2 to create a story pole.

2. Dry-lay the first course of five bricks—center them on the footing, leaving ⅜" spaces between them. Mark reference lines around the bricks with chalk.

3. Set the bricks aside and trowel a ⅜"-layer of mortar inside the reference lines. Set a brick into the

Cutting List

Each 96" bay requires:

Part	Type	Size	Number
Stringers	2 × 6	96"	3
Siding	1 × 6	72"	16

A. *Pour footings that are 4" longer and wider than the pillars on each side. This project calls for 16 × 20" footings.*

B. *Trowel a bed of mortar inside the reference lines and lay the first course. Create a weep hole in the mortar with a dowel to ensure the drainage of any moisture that seeps into the pillar.*

© Jan Boer

63

C. *Lay each new course so the bricks overlap the joints of the previous course. Use a jointing tool after every five courses to smooth the firm mortar joints.*

D. *Lay the final course over a bed of mortar and wire mesh, with an additional block added to the center. Fill the joints with mortar, and work them with a jointing tool as soon as they become firm.*

E. *Spread a ½"-thick bed of mortar on top of the pillar, and center the cap, using the reference lines.*

mortar, with the end aligned with the reference lines. Set a level on top of the brick, then tap the brick with the trowel handle until it's level.

4. Set the rest of the bricks in the mortar, buttering the mating ends with mortar. Use the reference lines to keep the bricks aligned, and make sure they are plumb and level.

5. Use a pencil or dowel coated with vegetable oil to create a weep hole in the mortar of the first course of bricks, so that any moisture that seeps into the pillar will drain away.

Step C: Lay the Subsequent Courses

1. Lay the second course, rotating the pattern 180°, so the joints of the first course are overlapped by the bricks of the second course.

2. Lay the subsequent courses, rotating the pattern 180° with each course. Use the story pole and a level to check the faces of the pillar after every other course. Use the story pole after every few courses to make sure the mortar joints are consistent.

3. After every fourth course, cut a strip of ¼" wire mesh and place it over a thin bed of mortar. Add another thin bed of mortar on top of the mesh, then add the next course of brick.

4. After every five courses, use a jointing tool to smooth the joints when they have hardened enough to resist minimal finger pressure.

Step D: Lay the Final Course

1. For the final course, lay the bricks over a bed of mortar and wire mesh. After placing the first two bricks, add an extra brick in the center of the course. Lay the remainder of the bricks to fit around it.

2. Fill the remaining joints, and work them with the jointing tool as soon as they become firm.

3. Build the next pillars in the same way as the first. Use the story pole to maintain identical dimensions and a 96" length of 2 × 2 to keep the spacing between pillars consistent.

Step E: Install the Top Cap

1. Select a capstone 3" longer and wider than the top of the pillar. Mark reference lines on the bottom of the capstone to help you center it.

2. Spread a ½"-thick bed of mortar on top of the pillar. Center the capstone on the pillar, using the reference lines. Strike the mortar joint under the cap so it's flush with the pillar. If mortar squeezes out of the joints, press ⅜"-thick wood scraps into the mortar at each corner to support the cap. Remove the scraps after 24 hours and fill the gaps with mortar.

Step F: Attach the Stringers

1. On the inner face of each pillar (the face perpendicular to the fence line), measure down from the top and use chalk to mark at 18", 36", and 60".

2. At each mark, measure in 6¾" from the outside face of the pillar and mark with the chalk. Position a 2 × 6 fence bracket at the point where the reference marks intersect. Mark the screw holes on the pillar face, two or three per bracket.

3. Drill 1¾"-deep embedment holes at each mark, using the bit provided with the concrete screws. The hole must be ¼" deeper than the length of the screw.

4. Align the fence bracket screw holes with the embedment holes, and drive the 1¼" concrete screws into the pillar. Repeat for each pillar, attaching three fence brackets on each side of each line pillar.

5. Measure the distance from a fence bracket of the first pillar to the corresponding fence bracket of the next to determine the exact length of the stringers. If necessary, mark and then cut a cedar 2 × 6 to length, using a circular saw.

6. Insert a 2 × 6 stringer into a pair of fence brackets and attach it with 1½" galvanized screws. Repeat for each stringer.

Step G: Cut the Section Arch

1. Cut 1" off the ends of the cedar 1 × 6s to create a square edge.

2. On a large, flat surface, such as a driveway, lay out sixteen 1 × 6s, with approximately ½" of space between them and the cut ends flush.

3. On the two end boards, measure up from the bottom and mark 64". Tack a 1½" finish nail into each mark, 2" from the edge of the board.

4. Draw a line connecting the nails. Measure and mark the center (48" from the edge in our project). At the center, mark a point 6" above the original line. This mark indicates the height of the arch.

5. Place a 96"-long piece of flexible PVC piping

against the two nails. At the mid-point, bend the PVC pipe until it meets the height mark. Tack a 1½" finish nail behind the PVC pipe to hold it in place, then trace along the PVC pipe to form the arch. Cut the arch, using a jig saw to cut along the marked line.

Step H: Attach the Siding

1. Run a mason's string 2" above the bottom of the fence line as a guide.

2. Attach the siding to the stringers, using 1½"galvanized deck screws. Maintain a 2" gap at the bottom of the fence, and make sure the boards are plumb. Use ½" scraps of wood as spacing guides between boards.

3. Repeat for each section of fence.

G. *Align cedar slats for a 96" section, and tack two nails on opposite sides, 64" from the bottom. Deflect a piece of PVC pipe against the nails, 6" up from the middle, and trace the arch.*

F. *Attach 2 × 6 fence brackets to the pillars, using 1¼" countersink concrete screws.*

H. *Attach the cedar slats to the stringers with 1½" galvanized deck screws. Maintain their order to properly form the arch top.*

Stone & Rail

This 36"-tall, rustic stone-and-rail fence is constructed in much the same way as the brick and cedar fence, but with stone rather than brick and simple 2 × 4 rails rather than siding.

Each pillar requires a footing that extends 6" beyond its base in all directions. Carefully plan the layout and sort the stones before you begin setting the stone. If necessary, use a stone cutter's chisel and a maul to trim stones or cut them to size.

TOOLS & MATERIALS

- Tools & materials for pouring footings
- Tape measure
- Level
- Wheelbarrow or mixing box
- Mason's trowel
- Jointing tool
- Stone cutter's chisel & maul
- Stiff-bristle brush
- Drill
- Paintbrush & roller
- Type M mortar

- Stones of various shapes and sizes
- Wood shims
- 2 × 4 fence brackets (6 per bay)
- 1¼" countersink concrete screws
- Concrete drill bit
- Rough-cut cedar 2 × 4s, 8 ft. (3 per bay)
- Paint, stain, or sealer
- 1½" galvanized deck screws

© Jan Boer

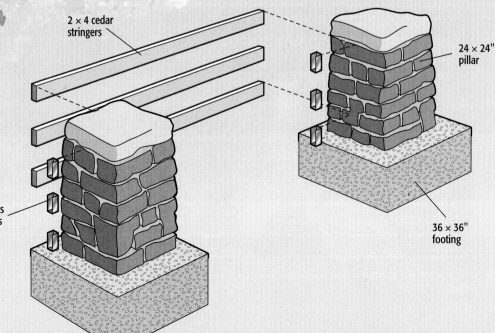

2 × 4 cedar stringers

Stringers brackets

24 × 24" pillar

36 × 36" footing

HOW TO BUILD A
STONE & RAIL FENCE

Step A: Dry-lay the First Course

1. Plot the fence line with stakes and mason's string (pages 18 to 19). For 72" bays between 24 × 24" pillars, measure and mark 18" in from the end of the fence line and then every 96" on-center.

2. Outline, dig, and pour 36 × 36" concrete footings (page 95). Let the concrete cure for two days.

3. Sort individual stones by size and shape. Set aside suitable tie stones for corners and the largest stones for the base.

4. Dry-lay the outside stones in the first course to form a 24 × 24" base centered on the footing.

5. Use chalk to trace a reference outline on the footing around the stones, then set them aside.

Step B: Mortar the First Course

1. Trowel a 1"-thick bed of mor-

tar inside the reference outline, then place the stones in the mortar, in the same positions as in the dry-run.

2. Fill in the center with small stones and mortar. Leave the center slightly lower than the outer stones.

3. Pack mortar between the outer stones, recessing it roughly 1" from the faces of the stones.

Step C: Lay the Subsequent Courses & Tool the Joints

1. Set each subsequent course

of stone in a bed of mortar laid over the preceding course, staggering the vertical joints.

2. On every other course, place tie stones that extend into the pillar center. Use wood shims to support large stones until the mortar sets. Build each pillar 36" tall, using a level to check for plumb as you work.

3. When the mortar sets enough to resist light finger pressure, smooth the joints with a jointing tool. Keep the mortar 1" back from the stone faces.

4. Remove any shims and fill the holes with mortar. Remove dry spattered mortar with a dry, stiff-bristle brush.

Step D: Lay Top Cap & Attach the Stringers

1. Lay a 1"-thick bed of mortar

on the pillar top and place the capstones. Smooth the joints as in Step C.

2. Mist with water regularly for one week, as the mortar cures.

3. On the inner face of each pillar, measure up from the footing and mark with chalk 12", 21", and 30".

4. At each mark, measure in 6" from the outside face of the pillar and mark, then line up the top and side edges of a 2 × 4 fence bracket where these two marks intersect. Mark the screw holes on the pillar, then drill a 1½"-deep embedment hole at each mark, using the drill bit provided with the concrete screws.

5. Align the bracket screw holes with the embedment holes, and attach with the 1¼" countersink concrete screws. Repeat for each bracket.

6. Measure the distance from a fence bracket on one pillar to the corresponding bracket on the next for the stringer size. Mark and cut 2 × 4s to size, using a circular saw.

7. Paint, stain, or seal each stringer, and allow to dry.

8. Insert stringers into the fence brackets and attach them, using 1½" galvanized deck screws.

Cedar & Copper

This cedar & copper fence can wear many faces: By staining the lumber and sealing the copper, you can give it a tailored, contemporary look; by leaving the lumber and copper unfinished, you can create a weathered, rustic look. Or, by painting the lumber and sealing the copper to keep it bright, you can create a fresh, crisp look.

Regardless of the finish you choose, this clever combination of cedar and copper pipe produces a durable fence with an interesting appearance. It provides security without completely compromising your view—in fact, we first saw a fence similar to this separating a swimming pool from a wildlife area.

The design was perfect for that situation: the height and the vertical nature of the fence made it difficult to breach, but the openness preserved the natural view beyond the fence line. Of course, regulations regarding fences around swimming pools vary by municipality, so it's especially important to check local building codes before planning such a fence.

TOP STRINGER CROSS SECTION

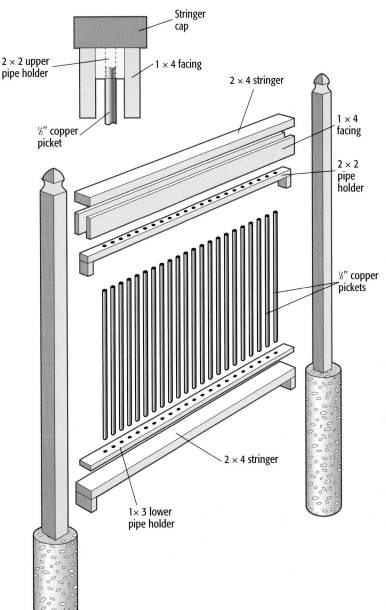

Stringer cap

2 × 2 upper pipe holder

1 × 4 facing

½" copper picket

2 × 4 stringer

1 × 4 facing

2 × 2 pipe holder

½" copper pickets

2 × 4 stringer

1 × 3 lower pipe holder

TOOLS & MATERIALS

- Tools & materials for setting posts (page 24)
- Paintbrush & roller
- Combination square
- Drill & spade bit
- Tubing cutter or hacksaw
- Chalk line
- Line level
- Framing square
- 4 × 4 shaped cedar fence posts (2 per bay)
- Paint, stain, or sealer

- Pressure treated, cedar, or redwood lumber:
  - 1 × 2, 8 ft. (1 per bay)
  - 1 × 3, 8 ft. (1 per bay)
  - 2 × 2, 8 ft. (1 per bay)
  - 2 × 4, 8 ft. (2 per bay)
  - 1 × 4, 8 ft. (2 per bay)
- ½" copper pipe, 10 ft. (11 per bay)
- 2½" galvanized deck screws
- 2" galvanized deck screws
- Stakes & mason's string

HOW TO BUILD A CEDAR & COPPER FENCE
Step A: Set the Posts & Prepare the Materials

1. Mark the fence line with stakes and mason's string (page 18).

2. Calculate the post spacing based on the contour of the land along the fence line (pages 21 to 23) and mark the post locations. Set the posts (pages 24 to 25), and adjust each post so that it is 66" above ground level.

3. Cut the lumber as described in the cutting list at right. Paint, stain, or seal all the pieces.

A. *Cut the lumber, then paint, stain or seal the pieces. Mark the fence line and set the posts.*

Cutting List			
Each 96" bay requires:			
Part	**Type**	**Size**	**Number**
Posts	4 × 4	10 ft.	2
Upper pipe holder	2 × 2	92"	1
Lower pipe holder	1 × 3	92"	1
Upper stringer supports	2 × 2	2"	2
Lower stringer supports	2 × 4	3"	2
Stringers	2 × 4	92"	2
Facings	1 × 4	92"	2
Copper pipe	½	55"	22

B. *Mark 4" on center spacing on the edge of a 1 × 2. Mark a center line on the pipe holder lumber, then transfer the spacing marks. Drill ½" holes, using a drill and spade bit.*

Step B: Make the Pipe Holders

1. Make a storyboard for the pipe spacing: On the edge of a 1 × 2, make a mark every 4"—you'll have a total of 22 marks.

2. For each bay, you'll need one 1 × 3 holder for the bottom of the fence and one 2 × 2 holder for the top. Use a combination square to draw a center line along the length of each pipe holder. Line up the storyboard along the center line and transfer the marks.

3. Drill a ½" hole at each mark, using a drill and spade bit. To keep the boards from splitting out, place the 2 × 2 over a piece of scrap lumber as you drill.

4. Calculate the number of pipes necessary for your fence line, and cut the appropriate number of 55" pieces of ½" copper pipe, using a tubing cutter or hacksaw.

Step C: Attach the Stringer Supports

1. At the first post, mark a level line across the inside face of the post, 2" from the ground. Align a 2 × 4 stringer support above that line and fasten it to the post with 2½" galvanized deck screws.

2. Using a chalk line and line level, mark a level po-

C. *Mark a level line and then attach a stringer support on the inside face of each post.*

D. *Fasten the stringers to the posts, then center the lower pipe holder on top of the stringer. Drive screws down through the 1 × 3 and into the stringer.*

sition on the opposite post. Use a framing square to transfer that mark to the inside face of the post, then fasten a stringer support to that post.

Step D: Install the Lower Stringer & Pipe Support

1. Set a 2 × 4 on top of the stringer supports and drive 2½" galvanized deck screws at an angle, through the stringer and support, and into the post.

2. Set a 1 × 3 pipe holder in place, centered on top of the stringer. Drive 2" galvanized deck screws through the pipe holder and down into the stringer. Add screws between every other pair of holes in the 1 × 3.

Step E: Install the Upper Pipe Holder

1. Mark a level line on the inside face of the post, 3" down from the flare of the post. Measure the distance between the top of the lower stringer and the bottom of the upper stringer support. Transfer that measurement to the inside face of the opposite post and draw a level line.

2. On each post, align a stringer support below the mark and fasten it to the post with 2½" galvanized deck screws.

3. Set a 2 × 2 pipe holder on top of the stringer supports and drive 2½" galvanized deck screws at an angle through the support and into the post.

Step F: Place the Pipes & Add the Facings

1. Working from above the upper pipe holder, insert a pipe into each hole and settle it into the corresponding hole in the bottom.

2. Position a 1 × 4 facing on the one side of the pipe holder, flush with the top of the 2 × 2. Fasten the 1 × 4 in place, using 2" galvanized deck screws. Add a second facing on the other side of the fence.

3. Center a 2 × 4 stringer on top of the structure; secure it with 2½" galvanized deck screws.

NOTE: Built one bay at a time as described, this design can accommodate a slight slope. If you have a more radical slope to deal with, refer to pages 21 to 23 for further information.

E. *Mark positions for the upper stringer supports and attach them to the inside faces of the posts. Add the upper pipe supports and secure them, using 2½" galvanized deck screws.*

F. *Insert the pipes into the holes in the upper pipe holder and settle them into the corresponding holes in the lower pipe holder. Add 1 × 4 facings, then top the structure with a 2 × 4 stringer.*

© Charles Mann

Walls

Wall. The word itself evokes visions of a barrier—tall, solid, and imposing. But in your yard, walls can't be defined in such a limited way. Landscape walls serve many purposes: They can define the property boundaries, separate living areas within the yard, and screen off unpleasant views or utility spaces.

With a temporary wall, you can create privacy and intimacy without building a permanent structure. On the other hand, if you want permanence, little could be more durable than masonry walls. Masonry walls, such as glass block, concrete block, stone or stone veneer, and can introduce new textures and patterns into your landscape.

Living walls are another striking option. In some spots, a hedge might be just the thing to create a dense visual screen, diffuse wind, or absorb noise. Trellis walls, such as the post and wire trellis or the framed trellis wall, provide beautiful backdrops for your favorite vines or lush border gardens.

Using simple building techniques, the projects in this chapter offer a wide variety of choices for practical, visually appealing walls. Properly constructed, the walls you build should last decades with little maintenance.

IN THIS CHAPTER:

© Charles Mann

Types of Walls

Before deciding what style of wall you want to build, take a close look at what purpose you want the wall to serve. Walls, in contrast to fences, do not necessarily enclose an area. But like fences, they can partially or completely block a view, define your property lines, or provide privacy. They can also prevent or direct movement between two areas.

And in smaller lengths, some structures you may not think of as walls, such as trellises and arbors, can serve as backdrops to your landscape.

If you'd like to define your yard but retain a natural-looking landscape, a tall, dense hedge may be the best choice. On the other hand, if you need to provide privacy and security, mortared block may be the most effective solution.

Generally, the purpose for your wall will dictate its size, but consider its setting and the size of your lot when you're deciding on dimensions. Local codes often set regulations regarding size, as well as acceptable materials, footings and other reinforcements, and bulding permits. Always check local building codes before beginning any building or landscaping project.

Temporary Walls

Painted canvas draped over copper pipe makes an inexpensive, easily-stored alternative to a fixed structure.

Living Walls

Whether spaced closely in a hedge or trained to grow over a trellis, plants create living walls that soften the texture of a landscape.

- Post & Wire Trellis
- Wall of Arbors
- Hedges
- Framed Trellis Wall

Block Walls

Concrete or glass, blocks produce sturdy, durable walls that are surprisingly easy to build. Low block walls are used mostly for effect, but full-size mortared block walls also provide excellent security.

- Mortarless Block Wall
- Mortared Block Wall
- Glass Block Wall

Stone Walls

With or without mortar, stone walls lend a sense of permanance to a landscape. Though more expensive and time-consuming to build than other types of walls, stone walls stand for decades as testimony to the builder's patience and craftmanship.

- Dry Stone Wall
- Mortared Stone Wall

Temporary Wall

Not everyone wants permanent walls or fences. But even if you want to preserve a view or prefer the look of a wide-open landscape, there may be times when you'd like a little more privacy. A temporary wall can create a special setting for an intimate dinner, provide some late afternoon shade on a deck or patio, or screen a sunbather from view.

For this project, we painted canvas and then stretched it across a frame made of copper pipe and fittings. To create texture, we used two colors of paint and a specialty roller. These rollers, which come with complete instructions, are widely available.

Hinge extensions—similar to the ones used for the copper gate (pages 126 to 129)—allow the wall to be folded for storage. Review the instructions and photos for the copper gate project before beginning this one.

HOW TO BUILD A TEMPORARY WALL

Step A: Construct the Frame

1. Measure and mark the pipe for the first section of the wall, according to the diagram at right.

2. Cut the copper pipe to length (page 127), using a tubing cutter. Sand the ends of all the pipes with emery cloth, and scour the insides of the fittings with a wire brush. Apply flux to all the mating surfaces.

3. Dry-fit the pieces of the frame. Solder joints, starting at the bottom and working toward the top. Do not solder the lower crosspiece to the frame.

4. Build the second and third frames.

NOTE: The center frame has hinge extensions on both sides.

If you have the time and talent, you can stencil a trompe l'oeil on the canvas.

© Jan Boer

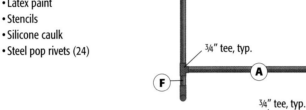

TOOLS & MATERIALS

- Tape measure
- Tubing cutter
- Wire brush
- Propane torch
- Caulk gun
- Spring clamps
- Locking pliers
- Drill
- Pop rivet gun
- ¾" copper pipe, 60 ft.
- ¾" copper tees (20)
- ¾" copper end caps (12)
- ¾" copper 90° elbows (14)
- ⅝ × ¾" brass flange bearings (8)
- Emery cloth
- Flux & flux brush
- Solder
- Canvas, 5 yds.
- Latex paint
- Stencils
- Silicone caulk
- Steel pop rivets (24)

Step B: Add the Canvas

1. Cut three 68" lengths of canvas. Paint the canvas, and let it dry completely.

2. Run a bead of silicone caulk along the center of the top crosspiece of the first frame. Center the canvas within the frame and press it into the bead of caulk; clamp the fabric in place until the caulk dries. Wrap the fabric around the crosspiece.

3. Run a bead of caulk along the lower crosspiece and clamp the canvas in place. When the caulk is dry, use a pair of locking pliers to turn the crosspiece within the fittings. Turn the pipe until the canvas is wrapped around the pipe and the fabric is taut across the frame.

3. Drill four evenly spaced pilot holes across each crosspiece. Secure the canvas to the pipe, using a pop rivet gun and steel pop rivets.

Cutting List
(totals for three 5 ft. frames)

Key	Part	Size	Number
A	Horizontal braces	38½"	6
B	Vertical braces	54¼"	2
C	Hinge sides braces	13½"	4
D	Middle hinge side brace	24¾"	4
E	Hinge sides braces	14½"	4
F	Legs	3½"	6
G	Feet	9¾"	12
H	Canvas	38¼" × 68"	3

A. *Mark and cut the copper pipe, then clean and flux the pipe and fittings. Assemble and solder the frames. Do not solder the lower crosspiece.*

B. *Paint strips of canvas and let them dry. Secure the canvas to the frame with silicone caulk and pop rivets.*

Post & Wire Trellis

Successful gardens often seem to be studies in contrast. Great gardeners blend and contrast plant forms, colors, and textures, using each to its greatest advantage. Texture is an important element of this design equation.

To create the illusion of depth in a shallow planting bed, designers recommend using a vertical display of fine-textured foliage as a backdrop for several plants with large, coarse leaves.

Although many trellises are designed to support a riot of flowers or a rambunctious layer of foliage, few provide an adequate showcase for the type of delicate texture required in this situation.

It may sound like a big challenge to build a trellis that accomplishes this mission, matches the average person's construction abilities, and falls within a reasonable budget, but this project is remarkably simple. By topping cedar posts with decorative finials and stringing a lattice of plastic-coated wire between them, you can create a trellis that would be ideal for many garden settings.

The best plants for this trellis are twining climbers with small leaves. Among annual vines you can try sweet pea or cardinal climber. Good perennial vines include trumpet creeper, English ivy, and winter creeper. You can put your climbers in the ground or select a variety that thrives in planters or pots. Be sure, however, that the plants you choose are well-suited to the light exposure they'll receive.

TOOLS & MATERIALS

- Tape measure
- Posthole digger or power auger
- Carpenter's level
- Drill
- Stakes & mason's string
- Reciprocating saw
- Wheelbarrow
- Trowel
- Hammer
- Wood sealer
- Compactible gravel

- Quick-setting concrete mix
- 8 ft. cedar 4 × 4s (2)
- Scrap 2 × 4s
- Deck post finials (2)
- 2 × 3 fence brackets (4)
- 8 ft. cedar 2 × 4s (2)
- 1", 1½" pan-head sheet metal screws
- 1½" screw eyes
- Plastic-coated wire or clothesline
- Small galvanized finish nails

HOW TO BUILD A POST & WIRE TRELLIS

Step A: Prepare & Set the Posts

1. Apply wood sealer to the bottom 2½ ft. of each post and let dry. For extra protection, let the bottom of the post soak in wood sealer overnight.

2. At the chosen site, mark the posthole locations by setting two wooden stakes in the ground, 59½" apart.

3. Dig the postholes 36" deep. Doing this job properly requires a posthole digger or power auger. Put a 6" layer of compactible gravel in the bottom of each posthole.

4. Set the first post into a hole. Take a carpenter's level and make sure the post is plumb on two

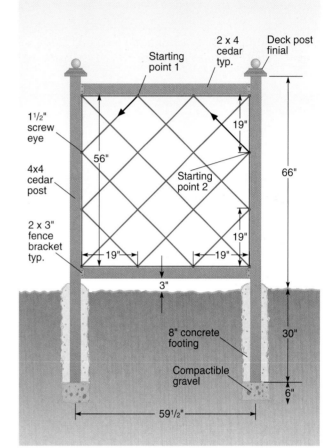

A. *Dig two 36"-deep postholes, and then add a 6" layer of gravel to each. Set a post into each hole, and align it. When it's plumb, use 2 × 4s to brace the post in position.*

B. *Pour quick-setting concrete into the postholes, adding concrete until it's slightly above ground level. Form the wet concrete into a gentle mound around the base of the post.*

adjacent sides.

5. When the post is plumb, use stakes and scrap pieces of 2 × 4 to brace it in position. Repeat the process for the other post.

6. When both posts are plumb and braced, use a mason's string to make certain the tops and sides are aligned. Adjust as necessary.

C. *On top of each post, set a decorative deck finial. Drill pilot holes and secure the finials with small galvanized finish nails.*

Step B: Pour the Footings

1. Following the manufacturer's instructions, mix quick-setting concrete in a wheelbarrow. Mix only enough for one post—quick-setting concrete sets in about 15 minutes.

2. Pour the concrete into one posthole, until the concrete is slightly above ground level.

3. Check the post one more time to make sure it's plumb and properly aligned.

4. With a trowel, form the wet concrete into a gentle mound around the base of the post.

5. Repeat the process for the other post, taking care that it's plumb and aligned with the first post.

6. Let the concrete set for one to two hours.

Step C: Install the Finials

1. Check the tops of the posts to make sure they're level. If not, use a reciprocating saw to trim one post until it's level with the other.

2. Set a decorative deck post finial on top of each post. Drill two pilot holes on each side and secure the finials with small galvanized finish nails.

Step D: Install the Stringers

1. Attach the bottom 2 × 3 fence brackets with 1½" pan-head sheet metal screws, 3" above the bottom of each post.

2. To make the stringers, measure the distance between brackets and cut two cedar 2 × 4s to length. Insert one 2 × 4 in the bottom set of brackets and attach it with 1" pan-head sheet metal screws.

D. *Attach the fence brackets 3" from the bottoms of the posts, using sheet metal screws.*

E. *Run wire diagonally between the screw eyes on the posts and stringers.*

3. Measure 56" up from the top of the first stringer. Install top brackets and fasten the second 2 × 4 to the top set of brackets.

Step E: Install the Screw Eyes & String the Wire

1. Starting in one corner where a stringer meets a post, make a mark on the inside edge of the stringer, 19" from the corner. Next, mark the inside face of the post, 19" from the corner. Repeat the process for the remaining three corners.

2. Drill pilot holes and attach screw eyes at each of the marked points. At the corners, angle the pilot holes at 45° toward the center of the trellis frame.

3. Using plastic-coated wire or clothesline, begin putting the trellis together by knotting the wire on the screw eye at the marked starting point. Feed it through the closest screw eye on the post and down through the screw eye below that. Following the diagram on page 79, continue stringing the wire in a diagonal, back and forth pattern, finishing at the lower screw eye on the opposite post.

4. Beginning at the second starting point (as indicated on the diagram on page 79), string a second wire. Thread it as described above to complete the opposing diagonal runs.

VARIATION: SIMPLE TRELLIS PLAN

1. You can build an easier, less decorative version of the Post & Wire Trellis without the stringers and the crosshatch wire layout. Start by following the directions for Steps A through C.

2. Measuring 1" from the inside tops of the posts, mark the location of the first screw eye. Then continue marking screw eye locations every 8" down the post, putting the last mark a few inches off the ground. Repeat the process for the other post.

3. Drill pilot holes and install the screw eyes, twisting them so that the "eyes" are parallel to the ground, not at right angles to it.

4. Attach the plastic-coated wire with a secure knot to one of the top screw eyes. Then feed the wire through the screw eye on the opposite side, then down through the screw eye directly below.

5. Pull the wire across to the second screw eye down on the opposite side, feeding it through and down to the screw eye directly below. Keep the wire as taut as possible at every run.

6. Continue this process until you reach the final screw eye, and then knot the wire securely.

HANGING BASKETS ADDITION

1. To make use of the outside or front edge of the posts, install decorative brackets for hanging plants. Position brackets along the side or front of the post as desired, centered along the post. Mark the screw holes and drill pilot holes. Each post should accommodate at least two brackets.

2. Attach brackets with the screws supplied, and hang planter baskets.

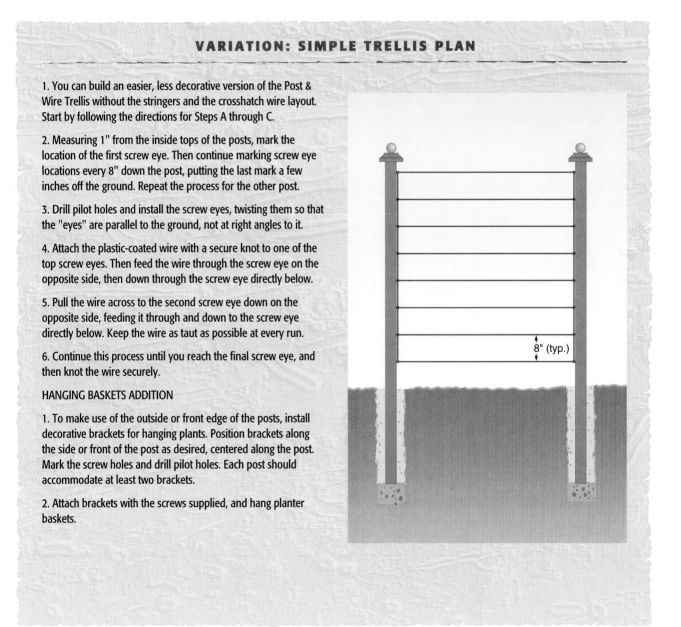

8" (typ.)

Wall of Arbors

Rather than acting as a barrier, this wall of arbors welcomes visitors with open arms. Planted with roses or flowering vines, it creates a luxurious, ornamental accent to your yard or garden.

Gracefully connected side-by-side, these arched arbors could, in addition to providing an accent to your yard, mark a property line or define an outdoor living space. And with well chosen plantings, they can either partially screen out or enhance a view, depending on your preferences.

Copper plumbing materials go together much like children's construction toys, so these arbors are fun to build. If you're new to soldering, this is a good project to learn on—the size is manageable and the joints don't have to be absolutely watertight. Just work carefully and remember that if you don't get the joints right the first time, the materials aren't wasted. You can reheat the solder, pop off and clean the fittings, and start again. You do, however, have to be precise about the alignment of certain pieces (page 84) so the arbors fit together well when you connect them to one another.

ARCH: TOP VIEW

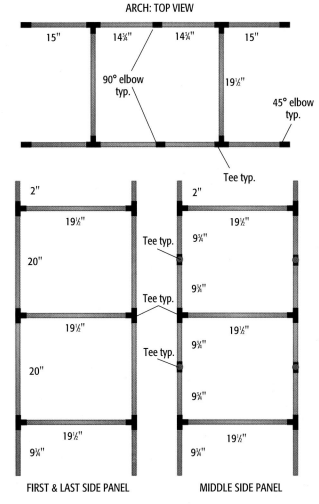

15" 14¾" 14¾" 15"

90° elbow typ.

19½"

45° elbow typ.

Tee typ.

FIRST & LAST SIDE PANEL

2"

19½"

20"

19½"

20"

19½"

9¾"

Tee typ.

MIDDLE SIDE PANEL

2"

19½"

9¾"

9¾"

19½"

9¾"

19½"

9¾"

Tee typ.

Tee typ.

TOOLS & MATERIALS

- Tape measure
- Tubing cutter
- Drill
- Round file (optional)
- Propane torch
- Hand maul
- Plywood scraps, at least 10 × 40" (2)
- 6 to 8" pieces of ⅜" dowel (4)
- 1 × 2s, at least 46" long (2)
- 1" deck screws (8)
- Wood glue
- ½" copper pipe (5 10-ft. sticks per arbor)
- ½" copper tees (20 per arbor)
- ½" copper 45° elbows (4 per arbor)
- ½" copper 90° elbows (2 per arbor)
- Emery cloth or nylon scouring pad
- Wire brush
- Flux & flux brush
- Solder
- #3 rebar, 36" sections (2 per arbor)
- Stakes & string

HOW TO BUILD A WALL OF ARBORS
Step A: Cut the Pipe & Build a Support Jig

1. Measure, mark, and cut the copper pipe, following the cutting list shown at right below. Clean and flux the pipes.

2. To build a support jig, start with two scraps of plywood at least 10" wide and 35 to 40" long. Draw a line down the center of each piece of plywood, then drill two ⅜" holes, 20" apart along the line. Glue a 6 to 8" piece of dowel into each hole. On each of two

1 × 2s, draw a pair of marks 42½" apart. Lay the 1 × 2s across the pieces of plywood, aligning the marks on the 1 × 2s with the lines on the plywood to set the exact spacing for the sides of the arch. Secure the 1 × 2s to the plywood, using 1" screws.

Cutting List
For each arbor, you need ½" copper pipe in these lengths:

Length	Quantity
15"	4
14¾"	4
2"	4
20"	4*
19½"	12
9¾"	12 or 20**

* For first and last Arbor

** 12 for first and last Arbor, 20 for each intermediate arbor

A. *Make a support jig: attach pieces of dowel to scraps of plywood, then use 1 × 2s as spacers to set the distance between the sides of the jig.*

B. *Dry fit the leg assemblies: alternate pipe and tees to form the legs, then add horizontal supports.*

Step B: Construct the Leg Assemblies

1. Slide a 9¾" length of pipe over the first dowel, add a tee, then alternate pipe and tees as indicated on the drawing on page 83.

2. Slide a 9¾" length of pipe over the second dowel, then alternate tees and pipe as indicated.

3. Fit 19½" lengths of pipe between pairs of tees to form horizontal supports.

4. Repeat numbers 1 through 3 to construct a leg assembly for the other side of the arbor.

Step C: Solder the Leg Assemblies

Disassemble the pieces and solder the joints in each leg assembly, working from the ground up. When the joints are cool, set the assemblies aside. NOTE: In order to connect the arbors, it's very important that you solder the open tees so they're exactly perpendicular to the plane of the leg assemblies.

Step D: Construct the Arch

1. Working on a flat surface, connect two 14¾" lengths of pipe, using a 90° elbow. Add a tee, then a 15" length of pipe to each side. Repeat to form a second, identical arch.

2. Slide a 45° elbow onto each dowel of the support jig, then slide the legs of the arches onto those elbows.

3. Add 19½" lengths of pipes between sets of tees, forming horizontal supports as indicated on page 83.

C. *Disassemble the pieces and solder each joint, working from the ground up.*

D. *Using 90° elbows, pipe, and tees, build the arch assemblies. Connect the arches with horizontal braces and tees.*

4. Disassemble the pieces and build the arch assembly, soldering as you go. When the joints are cool, set the assembly aside.

5. Put the leg assemblies back onto the support jig and fit the arch assembly into place; solder the joints.

6. Repeat Steps B through C to build as many arbors as necessary.

Step E: Install the First Arbor

1. Use stakes and string to create a straight line for the position of the arbors. Set the arbors in place, 19½" apart and aligned with the string.

2. Push down on the sides of the first arbor to mark the position of the legs onto the ground; remove the arbor. At two opposite corners, drive a 3-ft. piece of rebar about 18" into the ground. (CAUTION: buried utility lines are dangerous. Have your provider mark the utilities before digging any holes or driving anything deep into the soil.)

3. Fit two legs of the arbor over the buried rebar, firmly anchoring it in place.

Step F: Connect the Remaining Arbors

1. Flux the ends of a 19½" piece of pipe as well as the tees on the inside faces of the first two arbors. Set the second arbor into place, aligned with the strings and 19½" from the inside face of the first arbor. Add the horizontal braces that connect the arbors.

2. Mark the leg positions and anchor two legs on the second arbor.

3. Solder the joints on the horizontal braces.

4. Repeat this process to install the remaining arbors.

E. *Position the first arbor, and press its legs into the ground to mark their positions. At two opposite corners, drive 36" pieces of rebar 18" into the ground. Settle the arbor over the rebar.*

F. *Position and anchor the second arbor. Add horizontal braces, then solder them into position.*

Hedges

Hedges are a natural choice for creating landscape walls. Because hedges are living walls of individual shrubs, they easily blend into any landscape. Like fences and other nonliving walls, hedges can take many forms, depending on the purpose and style you have in mind. For instance, an informal hedge of flowering shrubs adds seasonal color, while a formal hedge of closely planted evergreens forms a dense screen that increases privacy.

Shrub choices generally fall into two groups: fast-growing or steady-growing. Carefully consider the pros and cons of each before selecting shrubs for a hedge. Fast-growing shrubs quickly form a solid hedge, but their rapid growth means that you'll need to prune them frequently in order to keep the hedge well shaped and healthy. Steady-growing shrubs require less frequent pruning, but take at least several years to grow into a solid wall.

To ensure that the shrubs grow into a dense hedge, determine their mature size and space them at about ¾ of this measurement. Check with a nursery before you begin planting—some shrubs require different spacing. The size of the excavation also has a tremendous influence on the success of your hedge. In most cases, you'll want to dig a hole twice as wide and just as deep as the container. However, if you have heavy soil, dig a hole that will position the top of the root ball slightly above ground, then mound the soil up to cover the roots.

Begin training the shrubs into a hedge by pruning them the first year. Taper the shrub so the bottom of the plant is wider than the top. Don't overprune—in general, it's best to prune within 2" of the last pruning.

HOW TO PLANT A STAGGERED HEDGE

The staggered planting method is the best choice for quickly forming an informal, living wall. It's also the preferred method if you're using shrubs that can't be planted close together. Although the hedge demonstrated here is straight, you can use a rope to lay out a curved hedge.

Step A: Dig Planting Holes

1. Use stakes and string to lay out the hedge's path.
2. On one side of the string, mark the appropriate spacing for a row of planting holes, then dig them.
3. On the other side of the string, mark and dig

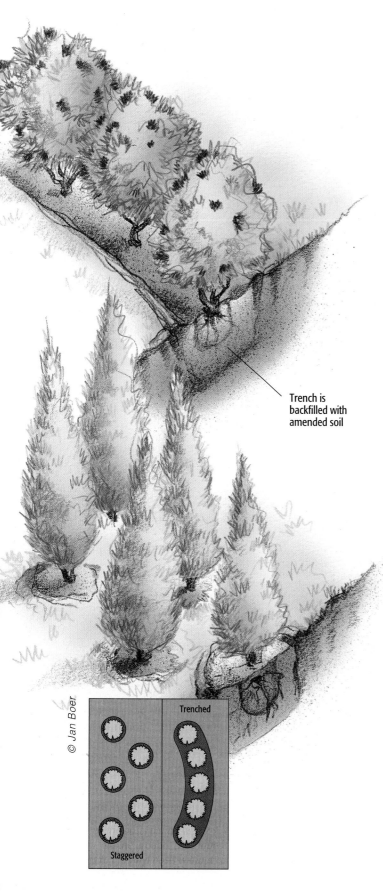

Trench is backfilled with amended soil

© Jan Boer

Trenched

Staggered

TOOLS & MATERIALS

- Shovel
- Stakes
- String
- Rope or hose
- Soil amendments
- Shrubs
- Mulch

another row of holes, staggered with the first row.

Step B: Install the Plants

1. Center a plant in the hole, positioning it so the root ball is at the desired depth.

2. Fill the hole ¾ full with amended soil.

3. When the hole is ¾ full, slowly add water, which will remove any air pockets. Finish filling the hole with soil and tamp it gently.

4. Apply 4" to 6" of mulch and water the shrubs.

HOW TO PLANT A TRENCHED HEDGE

Another option for planting a hedge involves digging a trench. This trench method works best if you want a formal or shaped hedge, and if you are willing to wait for the plants to grow into a solid screen.

Step A: Dig the Trench

Outline the path for a curved hedge, using a rope or hose. If you're planting a straight hedge, use stakes and string to mark the path. Dig a trench, twice as wide and just as deep as the shrubs' containers.

Step B: Install the Shrubs

Plant the shrubs one at a time, spacing them appropriately for their mature size. Hold each plant so it's centered and straight in the trench. Use the same planting technique described in the "Staggered Hedge" instructions, then apply mulch and water the shrubs generously.

Staggered Hedge

A. *Dig holes twice as wide and as deep as the shrubs' containers. Stagger the holes along both sides of the line.*

B. *Partially backfill soil around the plant, then water the soil. Fill the hole and apply mulch.*

Trenched Hedge

A. *Dig a trench twice the width and the same depth as the plants' containers.*

B. *Space the shrubs ¾ of their mature size apart. Fill the trench with soil and apply mulch.*

Framed Trellis Wall

This simple design creates a sophisticated trellis wall that would work in many settings. Part of its appeal is that the materials are inexpensive and the construction remarkably simple.

It can be used as a accent wall, a backdrop to a shallow garden bed, or a screen to block a particular view. As a vertical showcase for foliage or flowers, it can support a wide display of colorful choices. Try perennial vines such as Golden Clematis (*Clematis tangutica*) or Trumpet Creeper (*Campsis radicans*). Or, for spectacular autumn color, plant Boston Ivy (*tricuspidata*). If you prefer annual vines, you might choose Morning Glories (*Ipomoea tricolor*) or a Black-eyed Susan Vine (*Thunbergia alata*). The possibilities go on and on—just make sure that the plants you select are well-suited to the amount of sunlight they'll receive.

Depending on the overall look you want to achieve, you can paint, stain, or seal the wall to contrast with or complement your house or other established structures. Well-chosen deck post finials can also help tie the wall into the look of your landscape.

This project creates three panels. If you adapt it to use a different number of panels, you'll need to revise the materials list.

TOOLS & MATERIALS

- Tools & materials for setting posts (page 24)
- Tape measure
- Framing square
- Hammer
- Chalk line
- Line level
- Reciprocating saw or hand saw
- Paintbrush & roller
- Circular saw
- Drill
- Caulk gun
- Nail set

- Pressure-treated, cedar, or redwood lumber:
  - 4 × 4 posts, 10 ft. (4)
  - 2 × 4s, 10 ft. (3)
  - 1 × 4s, 10 ft. (12)
  - 1 × 1s, 10 ft. (12)
  - 4 × 8-ft. lattice panels (3)
- Paint, stain, or sealer
- 10d galvanized casing nails
- 4d galvanized finish nails
- 6d galvanized finish nails
- Construction adhesive
- Deck post finials (4)

A. *Set posts and let the concrete dry thoroughly. Snap level chalk lines to indicate the positions for the stringers. At the line for the top stringer, measure up 10" and draw a cutting line on each post.*

HOW TO BUILD A FRAMED TRELLIS WALL

Step A: Set the Posts

1. Mark the post positions 4 ft. apart, as indicated in the diagram at right. Dig holes and set the posts (pages 24 to 25). It's important to maintain the 4-ft. spacing between posts as accurately as possible.

2. On the first post, measure and mark a point 77" from the ground. Using a framing square, draw a level line across the post at the mark. Tack a nail in place along the line, and tie a chalk line to it. Stretch the chalk line to the opposite post, then use a line level to level it. Remove the line

Cutting List

Part	Lumber	Size	Number
Posts	4 × 4	10 ft.	4
Stringers	2 × 4	48"	6
Back frame			
Top & bottom	1 × 4	41"	6
Sides	1 × 4	72"	6
Front frame			
Top & bottom	1 × 4	48"	6
Sides	1 × 4	65"	6
Stops			
Top & bottom	1 × 1	48"	12
Sides	1 × 1	70½"	12
Lattice panels	4 × 8	48 × 72"	3
Post caps	1 × 6	4½ × 4½"	4

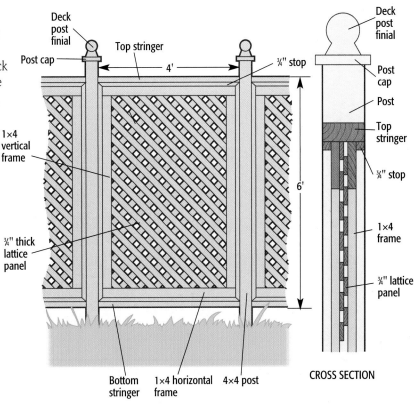

CROSS SECTION

level and snap a line across all 4 posts.

3. On each post, measure down 75" from the chalk line and draw a line across the post, using a framing square.

4. Mark a line 10" above the chalk line. Trim off the posts along these lines, using a reciprocating saw or hand saw. Paint, stain, or seal the posts, including the cut ends.

Step B: Prepare Pieces & Position Stringers

1. Cut the stringers, back and front frame pieces, stops, lattice panels and post caps as indicated on the cutting list on page 89. Paint, stain, or seal these pieces.

2. Transfer the level lines to the inside face of the posts, using a framing square.

3. Working between the two center posts, position the top stringer; make sure the top of the stringer is even with the marked line. Attach the stringer, toe-nailing it with 10d galvanized casing nails. Align the bottom of the stringer with the marked line and secure it in the same way.

Step C: Add Stops to the Back of the Fence Frame

Position a 1 × 1 stop flush with the back edge of the stringer and post, as indicated on the cross section on page 89. Drill pilot holes approximately every 8", then drive 6d galvanized finish nails through the stop and into the fence frame.

Step D: Set up the Back Frame

1. On a level work surface, position the pieces of the back frame to form a 4 × 6-ft. rectangle with butted joints. Measure the opposite diagonals. Adjust the frame until these measurements are equal, ensuring that the frame is square.

2. Run a bead of construction adhesive around the center of the back frame. Set the lattice panel in place, making sure it's square within the frame.

Step E: Attach the Front Frame

Set the front frame in place, with the joints butted in the opposite direction of those on the back frame. Square the frame as described in Step D, then secure the frame with 4d galvanized finish nails driven every 6". Sink the nails, using a nail set. Let the adhesive cure, according to manufacturer's directions.

Step F: Install the Framed Lattice Panel

1. Set the panel in place between the center posts, positioned firmly against the stops.

B. *Transfer the level lines to the inside of the posts, using a framing square. Install the first set of stringers between the center posts, even with the marked lines.*

C. *Add the stops to the back side of the fence frame. Drill pilot holes and nail the stops in place with 6d galvanized finish nails.*

2. Position 1 × 1 stops around the front edges of the frame. Push the stops in until they hold the panel snugly in place. Drill pilot holes approximately every 6" and drive 6d galvanized finish nails through the stops and into the fence frame.

Step G: Complete the Wall

1. Repeat Steps B through F to install the left and right panels.

2. Set a post cap over each post, positioned so that the overhang is equal on all sides. Nail the trim in place, using 6d galvanized finish nails.

3. On top of each post cap, draw diagonal lines from corner to corner, forming an X. Drill a pilot hole through the center of each X, then install a deck post

D. *Set up the pieces of the back frame, butting the joints. Square the frame, then apply a bead of construction adhesive along the center of the frame. Carefully set the lattice panel in place.*

E. *Set the front frame in place, butting the pieces in the opposite direction of the back frame. Drive 4d galvanized finish nails every 6" to secure the front frame to the lattice panel and back frame.*

F. *Set the panel in place between the center pair of posts. Add stops on the front side, then drill pilot holes and nail the stops in place, using 6d galvanized nails.*

G. *Install the remaining panels and add post caps to the posts. Add a deck finial to each post.*

Mortarless Block Wall

Far from an ordinary concrete block wall, this tile-topped, mortarless block wall offers the advantages of block—affordability and durability—as well as a flair for the dramatic. Color is the magic ingredient that changes everything. We added tint to the surface bonding cement to produce a buttery yellow that contrasts beautifully with the cobalt blue tile. However, you can use any combination that matches or complements your wall's surroundings.

Mortarless block walls are simple to build. You set the first course in mortar on a footing that's twice as wide as the planned wall, and extends 12" beyond each end. You stack the subsequent courses in a running bond pattern.

The wall gets its strength from a coating of surface bonding cement that's applied to every exposed surface. Tests have shown that the bond created between the blocks is just as strong as traditional block-and-mortar walls.

The wall we have built is 24" tall, using three courses of standard 8 × 8 × 16" concrete blocks and decorative 8 × 12" ceramic tiles for the top cap.

Choose a durable, exterior ceramic tile and use a thinset exterior tile mortar. Be sure to select an exterior grout as well.

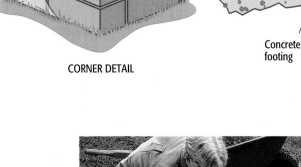

CROSS SECTION

Cap tile · Bullnose tile · Cap tile · Surface bonding cement · Three courses · Concrete footing

CORNER DETAIL

TOOLS & MATERIALS

- Stakes & mason's string
- Hammer
- Line level
- Tape measure
- Shovel
- Wheelbarrow or mixing box
- Hand maul
- Hand tamp
- 4-ft. level
- Hacksaw
- Chalk line
- Circular saw with masonry-cutting blade
- Masonry chisel
- Line blocks
- Mason's trowel
- Notched trowel
- Square-end trowel
- Groover
- Tile cutter
- Caulk gun
- Rubber grout float
- Sponge

- Small paintbrush
- Compactible gravel
- 2 × 4s for footings
- #3 rebar
- 16-gauge wire
- Vegetable oil or release agent
- Cement mix
- Sheet plastic
- Concrete blocks (end, half, & stretcher)
- Type N mortar
- Corrugated metal ties
- Wire mesh
- Surface bonding cement
- Fortified thinset exterior mortar
- 8 × 12" ceramic tile rated for exterior use
- Matching bullnose tile
- Tile spacers
- Sand-mix exterior grout
- Silicone caulk
- Grout sealer

HOW TO BUILD A MORTARLESS BLOCK WALL

Step A: Dig Trenches for the Footings

1. Lay out the location of the wall (pages 18 to 19), then use stakes and mason's string to outline footings that are twice as wide as the proposed wall. Measure the diagonals to make sure the staked outline is square, then use a framing square to make sure the corners are square. Adjust if necessary.

2. Strip away the sod 6" beyond the outline on all sides, then dig a trench for the footing. The bottom of the trench should be 12" below the frost line and roughly level.

3. Lay a 6" layer of compactible gravel subbase into the trench. Tamp the subbase thoroughly.

Step B: Build Forms & Add Reinforcement

1. Build and install 2 × 4 forms to outline the footings, aligning the forms with the mason's strings. Drive stakes along the outside of the forms to anchor them in position, then adjust the forms to level.

2. Make two #3 rebar grids to reinforce each

A. *Mark the wall and footings with stakes and string, then dig a trench for the footings.*

© Jan Boer

93

footing. For each grid, cut two pieces of #3 rebar 8" shorter than the length of the footing and two pieces 4" shorter than the depth of the footing. Bind the pieces together with 16-gauge wire, forming a rectangle. Set the rebar grids upright in the trench, leaving 4" of space between the grids and the walls of the trench. Coat the inside edges of the forms with vegetable oil or commercial release agent.

Step C: Pour the Footings

1. Mix and pour concrete so it reaches the tops of the forms. Work the concrete with a shovel to remove any air pockets.

2. Screed the surface of the concrete by dragging a short 2 × 4 along the top of the forms. Add concrete to low areas, and screed again.

3. When concrete is hard to the touch, cover the footings with plastic and let the concrete cure for 2 to 3 days. Remove the forms and backfill around the edges of the footings. Add compactible gravel to bring the surrounding areas level with the surface of the footings.

4. Let the footings cure for a week.

Step D: Lay Out the First Course of Block

1. Lay out the blocks for the entire first course. If you need to use less than half a block, trim two

blocks instead. For example, if you need 3½ blocks, use four and cut two of them to ¾ their length—this produces a stronger, more durable wall.

2. Use a level to make sure the course is plumb and a framing square to make sure the corners are square. Set a mason's string flush with the height of the course, along the outside of the wall.

3. Mark the position of the end and corner blocks on the footing, using a pencil.

4. Remove the blocks. Snap chalk lines to connect the end and corner marks for reference lines.

Step E: Set the First Course

1. Mix a batch of mortar, then mist the footing with water, roughly three or four block lengths from the end of the wall. Lay a ⅜"-thick bed of mortar on the misted area, covering only the area inside the reference lines.

2. Set an end block into the mortar bed at the corner. Place a stretcher block into the mortar bed directly against the end block with no spacing between the blocks. Place the next stretcher block in exactly the same manner. Use the mason's string as a guide to keep the blocks level and properly aligned.

3. Repeat this process, working on 3 to 4 ft. at a time, until the first course is complete. Periodically

TIP: MAKING ISOLATION JOINTS

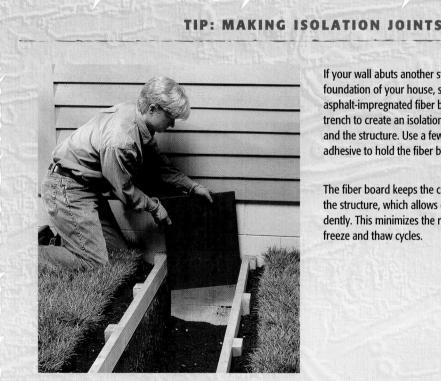

If your wall abuts another structure, such as the foundation of your house, slip a piece of ½"-thick asphalt-impregnated fiber board into the end of the trench to create an isolation joint between the footing and the structure. Use a few dabs of construction adhesive to hold the fiber board in place.

The fiber board keeps the concrete from bonding with the structure, which allows each to move independently. This minimizes the risk of damage during freeze and thaw cycles.

B. *Build 2 × 4 forms and stake them in place. Make rebar grids and put them upright in the trench. Coat the inside edges of the forms with release agent.*

C. *Fill the forms with concrete, screed the concrete level, then float the surface.*

D. *Lay out the first course of block, cutting blocks as necessary. Mark the ends and corners, then remove the blocks and snap reference lines.*

E. *Mist the footing with water, then lay a ⅜"-thick bed of mortar inside the reference lines.*

check to make sure the wall is plumb and level and that the corners are square.

Step F: Build Up the Corners & Ends

1. At a corner, begin the second course with a full-sized end block stacked so that it spans the vertical joint where the two runs meet. Make sure the block is level and plumb. If a block requires leveling, cut a

piece of corrugated metal tie and slip it underneath. If a block is off by more than ⅛", remove the block, trowel a dab of mortar underneath, and reposition the block.

2. Butt a full-sized stretcher block against the end block to form the corner. Use a framing square to make sure the corner is square.

3. Build the corner up three courses high. Keep blocks level and plumb as you go, and check the position with a level laid diagonally across the corners of the blocks.

4. Build up the ends of the wall three courses high; use half-sized end blocks to offset the joints on the ends of the wall.

Step G: Fill in the Subsequent Courses

1. Set your mason's string level with the corner and end blocks of the second course.

2. Fill the second course with stretcher blocks, alternating from the end to the corner until the blocks meet in the middle. Maintain a standard running bond with each block overlapping half of the one beneath it. Trim the last block if necessary, using a circular saw and masonry-cutting blade or a hammer and chisel.

3. Use a level to check for plumb and line blocks and a line level to check for level. Lay wire mesh on top of the blocks.

4. Install the top course, then fill block hollows with mortar and trowel the surface smooth.

F. *Starting at the first corner, stack a full-sized end block so it overlaps the vertical joint at the corner. Build the corners and then the ends three courses high.*

G. *Fill in the subsequent courses. On the next to the last course, lay wire mesh over the block, then install the final course. Fill the block hollows with mortar.*

H. *Apply the surface-bonding cement to damp blocks, using a square-end trowel. Smooth the cement and cut grooves as necessary.*

Step H: Apply Surface-bonding Cement

1. Starting near the top of the wall, mist a 2 × 5-ft. section on one side of the wall with water. (The water keeps the blocks from absorbing all the moisture from the cement once the coating is applied.)

2. Mix the cement in small batches, according to the manufacturer's instructions, and apply a ⅟₁₆"- to ⅛"-thick layer to the damp blocks, using a square-end trowel. Spread the cement evenly by angling the trowel slightly and making broad upward strokes.

3. Use a wet trowel to smooth the surface and to create the texture of your choice. Rinse the trowel frequently to keep it clean and wet.

4. To prevent random cracking, use a groover to cut control joints from top to bottom, every 48". Seal the hardened joints with silicone caulk.

Step I: Set the Tiles

1. Lay out the 8 × 12" ceramic tiles along the top of the wall, starting at a corner. If any tiles need to be cut, adjust the layout so that the tiles on the ends of the wall will be the same size.

2. Apply latex-fortified exterior thinset mortar to the top of the wall, using a notched trowel. Spread the mortar with the straight edge, then create clean ridges with the notched edge. Work on small sections at a time.

3. Place the corner tile, twist it slightly, and press down firmly to embed it in the mortar. Place each tile in this same manner, using tile spacers to keep the tiles separated.

4. Lay out the bullnose tile on each side of the wall. Again, start in a corner and make sure that the tiles at the ends of the wall will be the same size. Cut tile as necessary.

5. Apply mortar to the sides of the wall. Set the bullnose tile in the same way that you set the top tile. Tape the tile in place until the mortar dries.

6. Remove the spacers and let the mortar cure for at least 24 hours.

Step J: Grout the Tile

1. Mix a batch of sanded grout. NOTE: adding latex-fortified grout additive makes it easier to remove excess grout.

2. Spread a layer of grout onto a 4- to 5-ft. area of tile. Use a rubber grout float to spread the grout and pack it into the joints between tiles. Use the grout float to scrape off excess grout from the surface of the tile. Scrape diagonally across the joints, holding the float in a near-vertical position.

3. Use a damp sponge to wipe the grout film from the surface of the tile. Rinse the sponge out frequently with cool water, and be careful not to press down so hard that you disturb the grout.

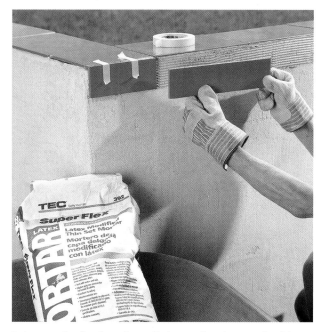

I. *Lay out the tile along the wall, then set it, using exterior thin-set mortar.*

J. *Grout the joints, using a rubber grout float. Wipe the film from the tile and let it dry. Polish the tile with a soft, dry rag.*

4. Continue working along the wall until you've grouted and wiped down all the tile. Let the grout dry several hours, then use a cloth to buff the surface until any remaining grout film is gone.

5. Apply grout sealer to the grout lines.

Mortared Block Wall

In some regions, mortared concrete block walls stand sentry at the borders of many yards. They're a durable, economical way to provide privacy and security. In some situations their utilitarian look is just what's called for, but in others a little decorative flair is in order. Adding decorative blocks as shown below or covering the blocks with stone veneer as shown on page 101 adds some style to these perennial favorites.

The wall we demonstrate here is 36" tall. If you're planning a wall taller than 36", you'll have to reinforce it by adding rebar and filling the block hollows with mortar. And, of course, a concrete block wall requires a footing that is twice as wide as the wall and reaches at least 12" below the frost line. Check your local building codes for installation requirements for both the wall and the footings

before you begin this or any block project.

There are three basic block types: **Stretcher** blocks have flanges on both ends and are used to build the body of the wall. **End** blocks are smooth on one end with flanges on the other. They are used for the wall ends and corners, with the smooth-face out. **Half-blocks** are also used to achieve the proper staggered block pattern. When using any type of block, make sure the side with the wider flanges is facing upward. These wider flanges provide more surface for the mortar.

Laying block is a matter of applying mortar to the footing and blocks and positioning them properly— proper positioning is the key to the strength and durability of a block wall. Keep in mind that although laying block isn't difficult, it is heavy work. If possible, recruit a friend or two to help you.

TOOLS & MATERIALS

- Tools & materials for pouring footings
- Stakes & mason's string
- Tape measure
- Hammer
- Pencil
- Circular saw with a masonry-cutting blade
- Chalk line
- Line level
- Wheelbarrow or mixing trough
- Mason's trowel

- 4-ft. carpenter's level
- V-shaped jointing tool
- Mortar bag
- Concrete blocks (end, stretcher, & cap)
- Type N mortar
- ⅜" wood strips or dowels

For Variation:
- Wire lath
- Self-tapping masonry anchors
- Stone veneer

HOW TO BUILD A MORTARED BLOCK WALL

Step A: Install the Footings

1. Plot the wall line with stakes and mason's string (pages 18 to 19). Outline the footings and measure the diagonals to make sure the outline is square. Adjust if necessary.

2. Dig the trenches and set the footings, as described on pages 93 and 94, steps A through C.

Step B: Lay Out the First Course

1. Test-fit a course of blocks on the footing, using end and stretcher blocks. Use ⅜"-thick wood strips or dowels as spacers to maintain even gaps for mortar. Cut blocks as necessary, using a circular saw and masonry-cutting blade.

2. Mark the ends of the course on the footing with a pencil, extending the lines well past the edges of the block. Snap chalk lines for reference marks on each side of the footing, 3" from the blocks.

3. Remove the blocks and set them nearby.

Step C: Set the Ends & Corners of the First Course

1. Mix mortar in a wheelbarrow or mixing trough, following the manufacturer's directions. (The mortar should hold its shape when squeezed.)

2. Dampen the center of the footing, then trowel thick lines of mortar, slightly wider and longer than the base of the end block.

3. Set an end block into the mortar, with the end aligned with the pencil mark on the footing. Set a level on top of the block, then tap the block with a trowel handle until it's level. Use the chalkline as a reference point for keeping the block in line.

4. At the opposite end of the footing, apply mortar, then set and level another end block.

5. Stake a mason's string flush with the top outside corners of the end blocks. Check the string with a line level, and then adjust the blocks to align with the string. Remove any excess mortar, and fill the gaps beneath the blocks.

Step D: Fill the First Course

1. Apply mortar to the vertical flanges on one side of a standard block and to the footing. Set the block next to the end block, leaving a ⅜" layer of mortar between blocks. Tap the block into position with a trowel handle, using the mason's string as a guide.

2. Install the remaining blocks, working back and forth from each end. Maintain ⅜" joints, and keep the course level, plumb, and aligned with the string.

A. *Dig trenches and pour footings twice as wide as the proposed wall.*

B. *Test-fit a course of blocks, placing end blocks and half blocks as necessary. Use ⅜" wood strips or dowels as spacers.*

3. When you reach the middle of the course, apply mortar to the flanges on both ends of the last block. Slide the block into place and line it up with the string.

Step E: Build Up the Ends of the Wall

1. Trowel a 1" layer of mortar along the top flanges of one end block of the first course. Scrape off any mortar that falls onto the footing. Start the second course with a half-sized end block, which will offset the vertical joints.

2. Build the ends up three courses high. Keep the blocks plumb and aligned with the mason's string.

NOTE: If the wall includes a corner, begin the second course with a full-sized end block placed to span the vertical joint formed at the junction of the two runs. Build up three courses of the corners as you build the ends. For further information on corners, see page 96.

Step F: Fill in the Subsequent Courses

1. Install the second course of stretcher blocks, using the same method as with the first course. When the second course is completed, use line blocks to set your mason's string for the new course line.

2. Scrape off excess mortar, and tool the joints with a V-shaped mortar tool.

3. Install each additional course of blocks by repeating this process. Finish the joints as each course is completed. Use a level to make sure the wall remains plumb.

Step G: Lay the Top Cap

1. Apply mortar to the top of the finished wall. Ease the end (and corner, if necessary) cap blocks into position—place them gently so their weight doesn't squeeze the mortar out of the joints.

2. Make sure the cap blocks are level and plumb, using a 4-ft. level.

C. *Lay a mortar bed, then set the end blocks. Stake a mason's string flush with the top outside corners of the blocks.*

D. *Apply mortar to the flanges on one end of each block (inset) and set the first course, alternating ends. At the center, apply mortar to both flanges of the last block and set it in place.*

E. *Start the second course with a half-size end block, which will result in staggered vertical joints. Make sure the wall remains plumb as you work.*

F. *Fill in the field blocks of the second course, alternating from one end to the other. Tool the joints with a V-shaped jointing tool, then install remaining courses.*

G. *Lay a bed of mortar along the top of the finished wall. Apply mortar to one end of each cap block and set it in place.*

VARIATION: APPLYING STONE VENEER

If a mortared block wall fits into your plans, but you don't like the appearance, you can set stone veneer over the finished wall.

Start by attaching wire lath to the entire surface of the wall, using self-tapping masonry anchors.

Next, apply a ½"-thick layer of mortar over the lath. Scratch grooves into the damp mortar, using the trowel tip. Let the mortar dry overnight.

Apply mortar to the back of each veneer piece, then press it onto the wall with a twisting motion. Start at the bottom of the wall and maintain a ½" gap between pieces. Let the mortar dry for 24 hours.

Fill the joints with fresh mortar, using a mortar bag. Use a V-shaped jointing tool to finish the joints.

Stone veneer can dress up the surface of a block wall. Veneer, which is lightweight and easy to handle, is available in many styles and colors. Shaped end and corner pieces greatly simplify the process of setting it.

Dry Stone Wall

Many homeowners —especially dedicated gardeners—dream of using low stone walls to form the boundaries of their yards or gardens. Sadly, many of them think those stone walls are destined to remain merely dreams. If you're one of those people, you'll be happy to hear that you don't have to hire a professional mason or learn to throw mortar in order to build a durable stone wall.

You can construct a low stone wall without mortar, using a centuries-old method known as "dry laying." With this technique, the wall is actually formed by two separate stacks that lean together slightly. The position and weight of the two stacks support each other, forming a single, sturdy wall. While dry walls are simple to construct, they do require a fair amount of patience. The stones must be carefully selected and sorted by size and shape. They must also be correctly positioned in the wall so that weight is distributed evenly. Long, flat stones work best. A quarry or aggregate supply center will have a variety of sizes, shapes, and colors to choose from. For this project you'll need to purchase a number of stone in these four sizes:

- Shaping: half the width of the wall
- Tie: the same width as the wall
- Filler: small shims that fit into cracks
- Cap: large, flat stones, wider than the wall

Because the wall relies on itself for support, a concrete footing is unnecessary, but the wall must be at least half as wide as it is tall. This means some stones may need to be shaped or split to maintain the spacing and structure of the wall.

To shape a stone, score its surface using a circular saw outfitted with a masonry blade. Place a mason's chisel on the cut and strike it with a hand sledge until the stone breaks. Always wear safety glasses when cutting or shaping stone.

TOOLS & MATERIALS

- Tools & materials for plotting a fence line (page 18)
- Shovel
- Circular saw with masonry blade
- Hand sledge
- Mason's chisel
- 4-ft. level
- Mason's trowel
- Safety glasses
- Stones of various shapes and sizes
- Capstone
- Type-M mortar
- Rough-textured rag

22 × 30" Flagstone cap

Tie stone position

Tie stone position

24" sloped trench for 1st course

HOW TO BUILD A DRY STONE WALL

Step A: Dig the Trench

1. Sort the stones by size and purpose, placing them in piles near the building site.

2. Lay out the wall site with stakes and mason's string (pages 18 to 19). Measure the diagonals to make sure the outline is square, and use a framing square to make sure the corners are square. Adjust if necessary.

3. Dig a 24"-wide trench, 4" to 6" deep, along the site. Create a slight "V" shape by sloping the sides toward the center. The center of the trench should be about 2" deeper than the sides.

Step B: Build the First Course

1. Lay pairs of shaping stones in two rows along the bottom of the trench. Position them flush with the edges of the trench and sloping toward the center. Use stones similar in height. If stones have

A. *Sort the stones by size and purpose. After planning the wall location, dig a V-shaped trench for the wall.*

B. *Lay the first course of shaping stones in the trench, adjusting them so that they slope toward each other. At corners, stagger the stones so the seams between stones are not aligned.*

C. *Build up the corner two courses high, with tie stones across the width of each just before they meet. Lay the rest of the course, working from the corner to the end of the wall.*

D. *Add the third course of stone over the second, using tie stones every 36", checking periodically with a level.*

E. *Once all the courses are in place, mortar the capstones to the top course of stone, then seal all the gaps between them.*

uneven surfaces, position them with the uneven sides facing down.

2. Form a corner by laying the last stone of the outer row so it covers the end of the stone in the outer row of the adjacent wall course. Lay the inner row in the same manner.

3. Fill any significant gaps between the shaping stones with filler stones.

Step C: Build Up the Corners

1. Lay the stones for the second course corner so they cover the joints of the first course corner. Use the same steps as forming the first course corner. Use stones that have long, square sides.

2. Build up the corner two courses high. Place tie stones across the width of each wall just before the corner.

3. Build the wall ends in this same way. Use stones of varying lengths so that each joint is covered by the stone above it.

4. Wedge filler stones into any large gaps.

Step D: Fill the Subsequent Courses

1. Lay the second course using shaping stones. Work from the corner to the end of the wall. Make sure to stagger the joints; stones of varying lengths will help offset them.

2. If necessary, shape or split the final stones of the course to size with a masonry saw or hand sledge and chisel. Carefully place the stones without disrupting the others.

3. For the third course, place tie stones every 36". Lay shaping stones between the tie stones and continue to place filler stones into any cracks on the surface or sides of the wall.

4. Continue laying courses, maintaining a consistent height along the wall and adding tie stones to every third course. Build up the corners first, and then build the courses with shaping stones, working from the corner to the end. Check for level as you go.

Step E: Set the Capstones

1. When the wall is approximately 36" high, check it for level.

2. Apply mortar to the center of the wall using a trowel. Keep the mortar at least 6" from the edges.

3. Center the capstones over the wall and set them as close together as possible.

4. Carefully fill the cracks between the capstones with mortar. Let any excess mortar dry until crumbly, then brush it off. After two or three days, scrub off any residue using water and a rough-textured rag.

VARIATION: SLOPES AND CURVES

If slope is an issue along your wall site, you can easily step a dry stone wall to accomodate it. The key is to keep the stones level so they won't shift or slide with the grade, and to keep the first course below ground level. This means digging a stepped trench.

Lay out the wall site with stakes and mason's string. Dig a trench 4" to 6" deep along the entire site, including the slope. Mark the slope with stakes at the bottom where it starts, and at the top where it ends.

Begin the first course along the straight-line section of the trench, leading up to the start of the slope. At the reference stake, dig into the slope so a pair of shaping stones will sit level with the rest of the wall.

To create the first step, excavate a new trench into the slope, so that the bottom is level with the top of the previous course. Dig into the slope the length of one and a half stones. This will allow one pair of stones to be completely below the ground level, and one pair to span the joint where the new trench and the stones in the course below meet.

Continue creating steps, until the top of the slope. Make sure each step of the trench section remains level with the course beneath. Then fill the courses, laying stones in the same manner as for a straight-line wall. Build to a maximum height of 36", and finish by stepping the top to match the grade change, or create a level top with the wall running into the slope.

If you'd like a curved wall or wall segment, lay out each curve, as demonstrated on page 20. Then dig the trench same as for a straight wall, sloping the sides into a slight "V" toward the center.

Lay the stones as for a straight wall, but use shorter stones; long, horizontal stones do not work as well for a tight curve. Lay the stones so they are tight together, off-setting the joints along the entire stretch. Be careful to keep the stone faces vertical to sustain the curve all the way up the height of the wall.

If the wall goes up- or downhill, step the trench, the courses, and the top of the wall to keep the stones level.

© Crandall & Crandall this page

To build a curved wall, lay out the curve using a string staked to a center point, and dig the trench and set stones as for a straight wall.

Mortared Stone Wall

The classic look of a mortared stone wall adds a sense of solidity and permanence to a landscape that nothing else can match. Although building a mortared wall takes more work than building a dry-laid one, in some cases, the tailored look of mortared stone is just what's needed.

Plan and position your wall carefully—making changes requires a sledgehammer and a fair amount of sweat. Before you begin work, check local building codes for regulations regarding the size and depth of the footings as well as construction details. And remember, in most communities any building project that requires a footing requires a building permit.

Plan to make your wall no more than 18" wide. Purchase a generous supply of stone so that you have plenty to choose from as you fit the wall together. Laying stone is much like putting a jigsaw puzzle together, and the pieces must fit well enough that gravity and their weight—rather than the strength of the mortar—will hold the wall together. Your stone supplier can help you calculate the tonnage necessary for your project, but you can make rough estimates with these formulas:

Rough Tonnage Calculations:

Ashlar: the area of the wall face (sq. ft.) divided by 15 equals the number of tons needed.

Rubble: the area of the wall face (sq. ft.) divided by 35 equals the number of tons necessary.

TOOLS & MATERIALS

- Tools & materials for pouring footings
- Stakes & string
- Line level
- Tape measure
- Wheelbarrow or mixing box
- Hand maul
- Masonry chisel
- Chalk
- Mason's trowel
- Batter gauge
- 4-ft. level
- Jointing tool
- Stiff-bristle brush
- Stones of various shapes and sizes
- Type N mortar
- ⅜" Wood shims

Step A: Pour the Footings & Dry-fit the First Course

1. Plot the wall line with stakes and mason's string (pages 18 to 19), then follow the instructions on pages 93 to 94, Steps A through C, to pour the footings. Let the concrete cure for 48 hours, then remove the forms and backfill around the footings. Let the footings cure for a week.

2. Sort the stones by size and shape. Set aside long, thin stones for tie stones. Using stakes, string, and a line level, set up a guide for the height of the first course of the wall.

3. Using larger stones, dry-fit the first course. Center a tie stone on the cement slab, extending from the front to the back. Lay out 3 to 4 ft. of the wall at a time, leaving ½ to ¾" between stones. Chisel or cut the stones as necessary.

4. Trace the outline on the foot-

ing with chalk. Remove the stones and set them aside, following the layout you have established.

Step B: Lay the First Course

1. Mix a batch of mortar, following manufacturer's directions. Mist the first 3 to 4 ft. of the footing with water, and then lay a 2"-thick mortar bed on the area.

2. Working along one side of the first course; set stones into the mortar bed. Wiggle each stone after you set it in place, then use the handle of a trowel to tap it down, just firmly enough to remove any air bubbles from the mortar bed.

3. Set the other side of the first course in the mortar bed. Fill the center with smaller stones and

mortar; leave the center slightly lower than the outer edges. If you need to reposition a stone, wash off the mortar before resetting it.

4. Pack mortar between the stones, keeping the mortar about 1" from the face of the wall.

5. Continue setting 3 to 4 ft. of the wall at a time until you've completed the entire first course.

Step C: Add Successive Courses

1. Adjust the string and line level to indicate the height of the next course.

2. Dry-fit the second course, 3 to 4 ft. at a time; add a tie stone at the beginning of each section. Stagger the vertical joints by setting one stone over two and two

over one.

3. Set the stones aside in the layout you have established. Lay a 2" bed of mortar over the first course, then replace the stones. Check the slope with a batter gauge, and use wood shims to support large stones so their weight doesn't displace the mortar. Keep the side relatively plumb, checking with a 4-ft. level.

4. When the mortar is set enough to resist light finger pressure (about 30 minutes), smooth the joints, using a jointing tool. Keep the mortar 1" back from the faces of the stones. Remove the shims and fill the holes. Remove dry spattered mortar with a dry, stiff-bristle brush.

Step D: Add the Capstones

1. Create a level, 1"-thick mortar bed on top of the wall. Center flat stones over the wall and tap them into the mortar.

2. Fill the spaces between stones with mortar. Tool the joints when the mortar is dry enough to resist light finger pressure.

Glass Block Wall

A translucent wall can be an elegant addition to a contemporary landscape. Glass block provides the feeling of privacy while allowing light to pass through. Glass may not immediately come to mind as a material for landscaping projects, but it's versatile, durable, and easy to work with if you keep a couple caveats in mind.

First, a glass block wall cannot function as a load-bearing wall. It has to be supported by another structure, such as a concrete block support column or an existing wall. Second, glass block can't be cut, so you have to plan your project carefully.

You work with glass block in much the same way you work with brick. Mix the special glass block mortar a little drier than standard mortar for brick, because glass doesn't wick water out of the mortar the way brick does. You can find glass block and installation products at a specialty distributor or home center. There are a variety of sizes, with different textures and

patterns that offer varying degrees of privacy. Bull-nose end blocks and corner blocks work well for finishing exposed edges; radial blocks are good for right angles or curves.

There are several items particular to this installation. T-spacers are plastic molds placed between blocks to ensure consistent mortar joints and help support the weight of the block to prevent mortar from squeezing out before it sets. Reinforcement wire adds strength and helps keep the courses properly aligned. And panel anchors are used to secure courses to the support structures.

Because installation techniques may vary from project to project, ask a glass block retailer or manufacturer for advice about the best products and methods for your project. If you'd like to build your wall on an existing foundation, such as a concrete patio, check with your local building department for structural requirements.

TOOLS & MATERIALS

- Tools & materials for pouring footings
- Tape measure
- Chalk
- Wheelbarrow or mixing box
- Mason's trowel w/rubber-tipped handle
- Level
- Wire cutters
- Jointing tool
- Sponge & pail
- Nylon- or natural-bristle brush

- Cloth
- 8 × 8" glass block
- ¼" wood spacers
- 6 × 8 × 8" concrete block
- Glass block mortar
- Glass block T-spacers
- Glass block panel anchors
- 6"-wide capstone
- Brick sealer
- Reinforcement wire
- 16-gauge wire

HOW TO BUILD A GLASS BLOCK WALL

Step A: Dry-Lay the First Course

1. Plot the wall line (pages 18 to 19). Outline and pour the footings, following the directions on pages 93 to 94, Steps A through C. Let the footings cure for 2 days.

2. Dry-lay the first course of the glass block over the center of the footing. Lay ¼" wood spacers between blocks to set gaps for the mortar joints.

3. Set a concrete block at each end of the course for the support columns, then center the glass block against the concrete blocks.

4. Mark reference lines on the footings, then remove the blocks.

Step B: Lay the First Course

1. Mist down the footings, then lay a ¼-thick bed of mortar inside the reference lines.

2. Set the concrete support block first. Make sure it is properly aligned so the glass block can be centered against it.

3. Begin at the concrete block, and set the glass block for the first course. Butter the leading edge of each glass block liberally to fill the recesses on the sides of both blocks. Use T-spacers beneath the blocks at the joints to maintain the proper joint spacing.

4. At the end of the course, set the concrete block for the second support column. Make sure it's properly aligned and level with the rest of the course.

5. Check each block with a level to make sure it's level and plumb. Make adjustments by tapping lightly with a rubber-tipped trowel handle (not a metal hammer).

6. Fill the gaps between the tops of the blocks with mortar. Set in the appropriate T-spacers.

Step C: Lay the Subsequent Courses

1. Apply another ¼"-thick mortar bed for the next course.

2. Lay the blocks for the subsequent course in the same way, beginning with the concrete block for the support column. Make sure the blocks of the new course are aligned directly on top of the one

A. *Dry lay the entire first course, with ¼" spacers between the blocks to set gaps for the mortar joints, then mark reference lines.*

B. *Set the first course in mortar, using T-spacers to keep the glass blocks evenly spaced. Gently tap with a rubber-tipped trowel handle to adjust.*

C. *Fill the gaps between the tops of the blocks with mortar, then position T-spacers. Apply a mortar bed, and lay the subsequent courses the same as the first.*

beneath. Use T-spacers in the joints to maintain the proper spacing. Repeat for each course, building the concrete block support columns as you lay each course, until reaching the desired wall height.

Step D: Add Reinforcement Wire

1. Add reinforcement wire across the entire wall, every other course.

2. Lay half (⅛") of the mortar bed, then set two par-

allel rails of the wire in the mortar, centered on the blocks. Overlap the wire by 6" where more than one piece is needed.

3. For corners, cut the inner rail of the reinforcement wire, then bend the outer rail to fit the corner. Tie the cut ends of the inner rail together with 16-gauge wire to secure it.

4. Cover the wire with the remaining half (another ⅛") of the mortar and build the next course.

Step E: Add Panel Anchors

1. Tie the glass block to the support columns using glass block panel anchors on every other course.

2. Use the same method as for the reinforcement wire to embed the anchors in the mortar, spanning the concrete block.

Step F: Tool the Mortar Joints

1. Smooth out the joints with a mortar jointing tool when the fresh mortar hardens enough to resist light finger pressure (within 30 minutes).

2. Remove excess mortar from the glass surface before it sets, using a damp sponge. You can also use a nylon- or natural-bristle brush, but take care not to damage the joints. Don't use steel wool or other abrasive materials that can scratch the glass surface.

Step G: Install the Capstone

1. Lay a ¼" bed of mortar on the final course.

2. Butter the leading edge of each capstone, and position it on the mortar bed. (Use capstone that is as wide as the cement block you've used in the

D. *Add reinforcement wire after every other course. Where more than one piece is needed, overlap the wire by 6".*

E. *Embed anchors in the mortar of every other course to tie the glass block to the concrete block support columns.*

F. *Tool the joints and remove excess mortar from the glass blocks for an even look, within 30 minutes of laying fresh mortar. Use a mortar jointing tool and a damp sponge.*

G. *Lay a ¼" bed or mortar, then add a single course of capstone to complete the wall.*

H. *Clean the glass block with a wet sponge to remove grit, rinsing the sponge frequently. Let the surface dry and remove any cloudy residue with a clean, dry cloth. After the mortar has cured two weeks, apply brick sealer to protect the wall from water damage.*

support columns.)

3. Tool the joints and remove any excess mortar with a damp sponge or nylon-or natural-bristle brush.

Step H: Clean, Cure & Seal the Wall

1. Clean the glass block thoroughly, using a wet sponge. Rinse the sponge frequently.

2. Allow the surface to dry, then remove any cloudy residue by rubbing the surface of the blocks with a clean, dry cloth.

3. Let the mortar cure for two weeks, then apply a brick sealer to protect the wall from water damage.

VARIATIONS: A MATTER OF STYLE

The wide variety of glass block styles and textures offers some options. You can use all one style of blocks or get creative by mixing styles. Consider making a checkerboard pattern with two complementary styles or even creating smooth "windows" within a textured wall.

The variety of available styles also offers options for topping your wall with something other than the traditional capstone. For the final course of a glass block wall, consider laying a different style of glass block from the previous courses. Bullnose end blocks and corner blocks are both good options.

Of Interest

Adding points of interest along a fence or wall can change the entire personality of a landscape. Look for ways to incorporate unexpected features.

- Paint a trompe l'oeil mural on a wall. To emphasize the dimensional effect, add plants that seem to extend from the painting.

- Attach eyehooks to a wall and thread rope or wire through them in an irregular pattern. Train vines to grow along the guidewires and keep them trimmed to create a random looking lattice effect.

- Prop a ladder against a fence and arrange potted plants on the steps. Add a few on the ground and several hanging nearby to fill out the scene.

- *Espalier* a tree against a wall by training its limbs to lie flush against the wall. Fruit trees, such as apple trees, take well to this age-old treatment.

(above) A trompe l'oeil scene surrounded by shutters gives the impression of a view beyond this solid wall.

(right) Imaginative use of rustic materials lends a festive air to this casual courtyard.

- Hang a window sash and a window box along the frame of a fence. Plant the window box with annuals and train vines to grow up and around the window sash.

- Attach a bracket to each post in a fence line. Hang a lantern or covered torch from each bracket. (Never leave candles or torches burning unattended.)

- Use a fence or wall to show off an unusual collection. Paint the background in an intense hue and then display a collection of interesting items, such as colorful miniature chairs, birdhouses, or bird cages.

- Fill sap buckets with annuals and hang them in an interesting pattern. Be sure the buckets have adequate drainage— make holes in them before planting, if necessary. And use lightweight potting soil to lighten the load.

- Secure a Victorian trim bracket to a wall or to fence posts. Suspend a lightweight hanging basket from each bracket.

- Bank container plants into a corner. Start with a small tree and stagger heights and sizes of plants to create a lively display. Or, top a low wall with planter boxes and go crazy with annuals and vines.

© Saxon Holt

(above right) Castor bean vines curl up this metal fence. Plants can warm up otherwise stark settings, soften harsh lines, or obscure undesirable views.

(right) Vivid color livens up a plain fence and gate. Here, cobalt blue sings in a Southwestern setting.

© Charles Mann

Gates

Although gates are uncomplicated, we ask a lot of them. These simple structures need to welcome family and invited guests at the same time that they turn away intruders. Succesful gates need to operate smoothly and keep their attractive appearance for many years with little maintenance.

A gate's allure and interest depend on its materials, color, and pattern, but its strength and durability depend on its structural design and how well it's built. No book can describe gates for every situation, but once you understand the fundamental elements of building a gate, a world of possibilities opens up. The style of your fence and existing landscape will strongly influence your decisions, but after reading through this chapter, you should be able to build a range of gates—from a dramatic trellis gate combination to a security-conscious arched gate.

Building a gate offers you the opportunity to stretch your imagination and make use of unexpected materials. For example, copper pipe and plumbing fittings, salvaged metal, and stained glass make quite a splash when recycled into gates.

As these projects show, gates give you a chance to make a statement. We hope they also show you that gates are about connection—not just to a fence or wall, but to the lives of the people on the other side.

IN THIS CHAPTER:

Types of Gates

The type of gate you build will depend on the purpose you want it to serve. Security gates should be tall, sturdy, and difficult to climb—which generally rules out horizontal siding. Gates in privacy fences typically need tall, closely spaced, solid siding.

As you plan your gate, pay particular attention to the width of the opening. If a gate is too wide, it will sag from the sheer load of its own weight. Typically, 48" is the limit for a hinged, unsupported gate. If your opening is wider than that, use a pair of gates.

Another important issue to consider is which way you want the gate to swing. Spend some time thinking about how the gate will be used, and make sure there will be enough space to maneuver the gate as well as an adequate place to stand while opening and closing it. This is especially important if the gate will be positioned at the top or bottom of a slope or steps.

The next step is to choose hardware for the gate, including hinges and latches. The clearance necessary between the gate and the posts will vary, depending on the hardware you select—check the hardware packages for specific requirements. If you're building a gate to fit an existing opening, adjust the gate's dimensions to allow the required amount of clearance. If you're planning a gate for a proposed fence, plan the placement of the gate posts so there is adequate clearance.

The best frame style for a gate depends on its size and weight. Z-frames are perfect for lightweight gate styles. Perimeter-frames provide support for larger or heavier gates. Both frame styles typically need cross braces to keep the gate square and to prevent sagging.

Basic Gates

The basic gate frame styles—perimeter and Z-frame—can be adapted to a wide variety of gate styles. By varying the shape, size, and spacing of the siding, you can create gates to suit almost any style of fence.

Gate with Stained Glass

This gate's eye-catching stained glass display allows light to filter through without sacrificing privacy. Thanks to the frame design, it's easy to adapt this gate to the dimensions of any stained glass window or other display piece.

Copper Gate

This elegant gate is ideal when set into a living wall or lightly used entry. The design ingenuously combines copper pipe and plumbing fittings to highlight an accent object. You can seal the copper to maintain its original color, speed up the development of a patina, or leave it to weather naturally on its own.

Arched Gate

Designed to complement a tall fence, this striking gate combines ornamental metal with the cedar. Positioned at eye level, the salvaged metal accent actually enhances the security function of the gate by allowing you to see who's approaching.

Trellis Gate Combination

Designed to support a lush bower, this trellis gate combination provides a dramatic and welcoming entry. While it's certainly more time-consuming to construct than a basic gate, the design is deceptively simple, and its beauty makes it well worth the effort.

Basic Gates

If you understand the basic elements of gate construction, you can build a sturdy gate to suit almost any situation. The gates shown here illustrate the fundamental elements of a well-built gate.

To begin with, adequate distribution of the gate's weight is critical to its operation. Because the posts bear most of a gate's weight, they're set at least 12" deeper than fence posts. Or, depending on building codes in your area, they may need to be set below the frost line in substantial concrete footings.

However they're set, the posts must be plumb. A sagging post can be reinforced by attaching a sag rod at the top of the post and running it diagonally to the lower end of the next post. Tighten the knuckle in the middle until the post is properly aligned. A caster can be used with heavy gates over smooth surfaces to assist with the weight load.

The frame also plays an important part in properly distributing the gate's weight. The two basic gate frames featured here are the foundation for many gate designs. A **Z-frame gate** is ideal for a light, simple gate. This frame consists of a pair of horizontal braces with a diagonal brace running between them. A *perimeter-frame gate* is necessary for a heavier or more elaborate gate. It employs a solid, four-cornered frame with a diagonal brace attached at opposite corners.

In both styles, the diagonal brace must run from the bottom of the hinge-side to the top of the latch-side, to provide support and keep the gate square.

There are a multitude of hinge, latch, and handle styles available. Whichever you choose, purchase the largest hinges available that are in proportion with your gate, and a latch or handle appropriate for the gate's purpose.

Z frame

Perimeter frame

© Jerry Pavia

TOOLS & MATERIALS

- Tape measure
- Level
- Framing square
- Circular saw
- Paintbrush
- Drill
- Spring clamps
- Jig saw
- Combination square

- Pressure-treated, cedar, or redwood lumber as needed:
  - 1 × 2s
  - 2 × 4s
- Paint, stain, or sealer
- Hinge hardware
- Gate handle or latch
- 2" galvanized deck screws
- 2½" galvanized deck screws

HOW TO BUILD A Z-FRAME GATE

Step A: Calculate the Width & Cut the Braces

1. Check both gate posts on adjacent sides for plumb, using a level. If a post is not plumb, reinforce it with a sag rod. When both posts are plumb, measure the opening between them.

2. Consult the packaging on your hinge and latch hardware for the clearance necessary between the frame and gate posts. Subtract this figure from the measurement of the opening. The result will be the finished wide of the gate. Cut 2 × 4s to this length for the frame's horizontal braces.

3. Paint, stain, or seal the lumber for the frame and as well as the siding for the gate and let it dry completely.

Step B: Attach the Diagonal Brace

1. On the fence, measure the distance from the bottom of the upper stringer to the top of the lower stringer. Cut two pieces of scrap 2 × 4 to this length to use as temporary supports.

2. On a flat work surface, lay out the frame, placing the temporary supports between the braces. Square the corners of the frame, using a framing square.

3. Place a 2 × 4 diagonally from one end of the lower brace across to the opposite end of the upper brace. Mark and cut the brace, using a circular saw.

4. Remove the temporary supports, and toenail the brace into position, using 2½" galvanized deck screws.

Step C: Apply the Siding

1. Position the frame so the diagonal brace runs from the bottom of the hinge side to the top of the latch side, then plan the lay out of the siding to match the position and spacing of the fence siding. If the final board needs to be trimmed, divide the difference and trim two boards instead. Use these equally trimmed boards as the first and last pieces of siding.

2. Clamp a scrap 2 × 4 flush against the bottom

A. *Make sure the gate posts are plumb, then measure the distance between them and calculate the dimensions of the gate.*

B. *Place a 2 × 4 diagonally across the temporary frame, from the lower corner of the hinge-side, to the upper latch-side corner, and mark the cutting lines.*

119

C. *Align the end boards of the siding flush with the edge of the frame and attach with screws. Using spacers, position and attach the remaining siding to the frame.*

D. *Shim the gate into place. Mark the position of the hardware on the gate and gate posts, drill pilot holes and attach the hardware.*

brace as a placement guide. Align the first and last boards, flush with the ends of the braces. Attach these two boards to the horizontal braces, using pairs of 2" galvanized deck screws.

2. Attach the rest of the siding, using spacers as necessary.

Step D: Hang the Gate

1. Shim the gate into position and make sure it will swing freely. Remove the gate.

2. Measure and mark the hinge positions on the gate. Drill pilot holes, and secure the hinges to the gate using the screws provided with the hardware.

3. If your latch hardware doesn't include a catch, add a stop on the latch-side post. Clamp a 1 × 2 in place, then shim the gate back into position, centered within the opening. Use a level to make sure that the gate is level and plumb, and that the stop is properly positioned. Drill pilot holes and secure the stop to the post, using 2" galvanized deck screws.

4. With the gate shimmed into position, mark the hinge-side post to indicate the hinge screw locations, then drill pilot holes. Fasten the hinges to the post, using the screws provided with the hardware.

5. Install the latch hardware to the opposite gate post and the catch to the gate, according to the manufacturer's instructions.

HOW TO BUILD A PERIMETER FRAME GATE
Step A: Build the Gate Frame

1. Determine the gate width and cut the horizontal braces, as for a Z-frame gate (page 119, Step A).

2. On the fence line, measure the distance from the bottom of the upper stringer, to the top of the lower stringer. Cut two pieces of 2 × 4 to this length for the vertical braces.

3. Paint, stain, or seal the lumber for the gate and siding, then let it dry thoroughly.

4. Position the pieces of the frame and measure from one corner to the diagonally opposite corner. Repeat at the opposite corners. Adjust the pieces until these measurements are equal, which indicates that the frame is square. Secure each joint, using 2½" galvanized deck screws.

Step B: Attach the Diagonal Brace

1. Position the frame on a 2 × 4 set on edge, running diagonally from the lower corner of the hinge-side to the opposite latch-side corner. Support the frame with 2 × 4 scraps underneath the opposing corners, if necessary.

2. Make sure the frame is square, and scribe the corners of the frame on the board. Transfer the cut marks to the face of the 2 × 4, using a combination square. Cut with a circular saw, making sure to set

A. *Determine the lengths of the horizontal and vertical braces of the frame. Lay out the frame, check it for square, and secure the joints with 2½" galvanized deck screws.*

B. *Scribe the opposite corners of the frame on the 2 × 4 diagonal brace. Cut the brace, using a circular saw with the blade adjusted for the appropriate bevel angle. Toenail the brace in place.*

the saw blade to the appropriate bevel angle.

3. Toenail the brace into position, using 2½" galvanized deck screws.

Step C: Attach the Siding

1. Lay out the siding on the frame, making sure that the diagonal brace runs up from the bottom hinge-side corner to the opposite top latch-side corner. Use wood scraps the same width as the gaps between the pickets in the fence line for spacing. If a board must be ripped to fit, rip the first and last boards to the same width.

2. Measure down from the top of the first and last boards and mark the height they will rise above the upper horizontal brace. Align the boards flush with the edges of the vertical braces, with the reference marks meeting the top edge of the upper horizontal brace. Attach each end board to each horizontal brace with 2" galvanized deck screws.

3. Clamp a scrap 2 × 4 flush against the bottom of the end boards as a guide. Align the rest of the siding, with the scraps used for spacing. Attach each board with 2" galvanized nails.

4. Paint, stain, or seal the gate and allow it to dry thoroughly. Mount the hardware and hang the gate as you would a Z-frame gate (opposite page).

C. *Secure the first and last siding boards to the frame, aligning them flush with the edges. Using scrap wood as spacers, attach the remaining siding.*

Gate with Stained Glass

This gate design started with a stained glass piece we wanted to showcase and grew from there. We know it's unlikely that you'll find a piece with the same dimensions, so we designed a structure that's easy to adapt. Basically, you need to build the frame, cut an opening, and use angle iron to hold your stained glass in place.

The beauty of this gate lies not only in the particular stain glass you choose to display, but also in the opportunity to make it uniquely your own creation. We've chosen a picket shape that reflects the diamond design in our stained glass piece, but any combination that appeals to you can be made to work.

Although this design includes a catch on the latch side post to keep the gate from swinging through the posts, a stained glass inset may not be a great choice for a gate that will be frequently used by young children. In that case, you could use an acrylic panel that mimics stained glass or showcase a completely different type of accent piece.

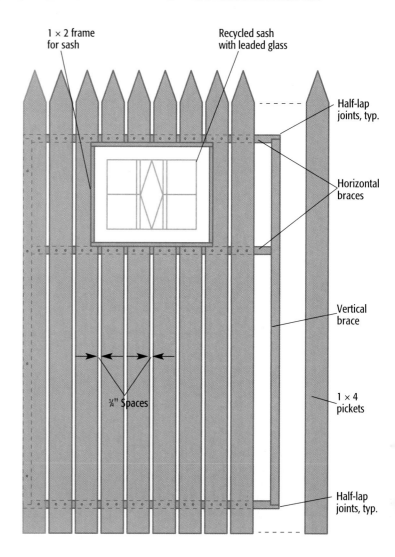

Labels on diagram:
- 1 × 2 frame for sash
- Recycled sash with leaded glass
- Half-lap joints, typ.
- Horizontal braces
- Vertical brace
- 1 × 4 pickets
- Half-lap joints, typ.
- ¾" Spaces

TOOLS & MATERIALS

- Tape measure
- Circular saw
- Paintbrush
- Hammer
- Chisel
- Drill
- Screwdriver
- Framing square
- Level
- Paint. stain, or sealer

- Pressure-treated, cedar, or redwood lumber:
  ¾" trim 8 ft.
  1 × 4s, 6 ft. (10)
  2 × 4s, 10 ft. (3)
- 1½" galvanized deck screws
- 2½" galvanized deck screws
- Angle irons (8)
- Galvanized 4d finish nails
- Hinge & latch hardware

HOW TO BUILD A GATE WITH STAINED GLASS
Step A: Prepare the Lumber & Build the Frame

1. Measure the opening between the gate posts and determine the finished size of your gate. Compare your actual dimensions to those in the cutting list at right and make any necessary adjustments. Cut the lumber for the gate.

2. Paint, stain, or seal the pieces on all sides and edges. Let them dry thoroughly.

3. Lay out the parts of the frame and mark the cutting lines for the half-lap joints (see diagram at right). To make a half-lap joint, set the depth of a circular saw to ¾" and cut along the marked line; make a cut approximately every ⅛ to ¼", working

A. *Lay out the frame, then mark and cut the lap joints. Assemble the frame, check it for square, and secure the joints with screws.*

© Jan Boer

Cutting List

Part	Type	Length	Number
Frame			
Horizontal braces	2 × 4	41¾"	2
	2 × 4	38¾"	1
Vertical braces	2 × 4	62½"	2
Trim			
Horizontal	¾"	22"	2
Vertical	¾"	15¾"	2
Siding Slats	1 × 4	72"	10

B. *Mark the position for the middle brace, then screw it in place, working through the face of the frame and into the brace.*

C. *Secure the first piece of siding to the frame, aligning it to be flush with the left edge of the frame. Using a 1 × 4 as a spacer, add the remaining siding.*

from the end of the board or joint area back toward that first cut. Remove the waste material and smooth the cut surface, using a hammer and chisel. Repeat with each of the marked joints.

4. Position the pieces of the outer frame and measure from one corner to the diagonally opposite corner. Repeat at the opposite corners. Adjust the pieces until these measurements are equal, which indicates that the frame is square. Secure each joint, using 1½" galvanized deck screws.

Step B: Add the Middle Brace

Measure the stained glass window you have chosen; add 1½" to this measurement. Measure down from the bottom edge of the top brace, and mark this distance on the inside face of each side of the frame. Carefully align the top of the middle brace with these marks. Drive three 2½" galvanized deck screws through the face of each side of the frame and into the brace.

Step C: Attach the Siding

1. Shape the top of the pickets as desired (page 45). Draw a reference mark 6" down from the top of each picket.

2. Place a picket on top of the frame, the left edge of the picket flush with the left edge of the frame. Adjust the picket so the reference line is even with the top edge of the frame's first horizontal brace. Drill pilot holes and attach the picket to the frame, using 1½" galvanized deck screws driven every 6".

3. Set a scrap 1 × 4 on edge and hold it flush against the attached picket. Position a new picket

flush against the spacer and screw it in place; drive two screws into each of the frame's horizontal braces. Reposition the spacer and continue until all the pickets are in place.

Step D: Cut Out the Display Area

1. From the back of the gate, set the stained glass piece in place within the frame. Measure to make sure the piece is centered within the frame, then mark the four corners. Remove the stained glass and drill a hole at each mark.

2. Turn the gate over and draw lines to connect the holes. Use a framing square and tape measure to make sure the lines create an opening that is square and centered within the frame.

3. Set the depth on a circular saw to ¾" (the thickness of the pickets), and cut along the marked lines. Remove the siding in the cut-out area.

Step E: Install the Display Piece

1. Attach two pieces of angle iron to each corner of the frame of the stained glass, using 1½" galvanized deck screws. Make sure the top of each angle iron is flush with the top of the frame.

2. Position the stained glass piece within the opening, aligning the front edge of the frame with the front edge of the pickets. Secure the stained glass piece by driving screws through the angle iron and into the frame.

Step F: Add Decorative Trim

Set the decorative trim in place, concealing the joints between the pickets and the frame of the

D. *Position the stained glass piece within the frame and drill holes to mark the corners. Connect the corners and use a circular saw to cut out the opening.*

E. *Attach angle irons to the display piece; drive screws through the angle iron and into the frame to secure the display piece.*

F. *Cut trim boards to fit and nail them into position to cover the gaps between the pickets and the display piece.*

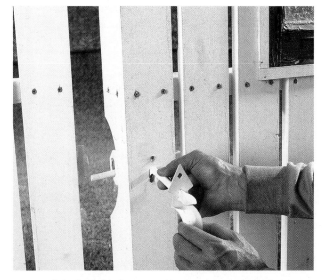

G. *Install the latch hardware on the gate post, then mark the catch positions on the gate; install the catch on the gate siding.*

stained glass piece. Drill pilot holes and carefully nail the trim in place, using galvanized finish nails.

Step G: Hang the Gate

1. Mount the hinges on the gate. Measure and mark the hinge positions. Drill pilot holes and drive screws to secure the hinges to the gate.

2. Shim the gate into position, centered within the opening. Use a level to make sure the gate is level and plumb. Mark the post to indicate the hinge screw positions, then drill pilot holes. Fasten the hinges to the post, using the screws provided with the hinge hardware (page 120).

3. Position the catch hardware on the opposite post. Mark the screw positions and drill pilot holes; drive screws to secure the latch in place.

4. Mark the latch positions on the gate. Drill pilot holes and secure the catch, using the screws provided with the hardware.

Copper Gate

This copper gate is an example of how ordinary materials can be used in extraordinary ways. Despite its elegant appearance, the gate actually is nothing more than simple combinations of copper pipe and fittings and a few pieces of inexpensive hardware.

The best setting for this gate is one in which it is largely ornamental. Although it's sturdy and fully operational, it isn't meant to provide security or to handle a constant flow of traffic in and out of your yard. However, set into a living wall or a section of fence where it receives light use, it can provide decades of service.

Copper pipe and fittings are intended to be exposed to water, heat, and cold, so they're entirely suited to outdoor use. The finish can be protected to maintain the bright color or allowed to develop a patina. To maintain the original color, spray the new copper with an acrylic sealer. On the other hand, if you don't want to wait for the patina to develop on its own, rub the finished piece with the cut face of a lemon or a tomato—the acid will speed the chemical process that creates the patina.

We used a copper watering can for an accent piece, but there's really no limit to what you could choose. If an object appeals to you and can be wired or soldered securely into place, you can make it work. You may have to adjust the dimensions of the display frame, but that's a simple matter of making a few calculations before you begin cutting the copper.

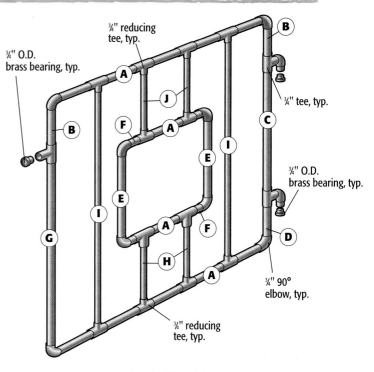

¾" reducing tee, typ.

¾" O.D. brass bearing, typ.

¾" tee, typ.

¾" O.D. brass bearing, typ.

¾" 90° elbow, typ.

¾" reducing tee, typ.

TOOLS & MATERIALS

- Tape measure
- Tubing cutter
- Paintbrush
- 4-ft. level
- Reciprocating saw or hand saw
- Locking pliers or pipe wrench
- Drill
- Emery cloth
- Wire brush
- Flux
- Solder
- Propane torch
- 4 × 4 posts, 8 ft. (2)
- Paint, stain, or sealer
- Tools & materials for setting posts (page 24)

- Deck post cap & finial
- ¾" copper pipe, 20 ft.
- ½" copper pipe, 10 ft.
- ⅝ × ¾ × 1 brass flange bearings (3)
- ¾" 90° elbows (10)
- ¾ to ½" reducing tees (12)
- ¾" tees (3)
- Lag screwhinges for chain link fence (2)
- ⅜" flexible copper tubing
- 8-gauge copper wire (about 8")
- Copper watering can
- 16-gauge copper wire (about 24")
- Galvanized finishing nails

CUTTING LIST

Key	Part	Size	Number
A	¾" pipe	6½"	12
B	¾" pipe	6"	2
C	¾" pipe	23¾"	1
D	¾" pipe	5"	1
E	¾" pipe	12½"	2
F	¾" pipe	2½"	4
G	¾" pipe	29½"	1
H	½" pipe	10"	2
I	½" pipe	36¾"	2
J	½" pipe	12¼"	2

HOW TO BUILD A COPPER GATE

Step A: Cut the Copper Parts

1. Measure and mark the pipe, according to the cutting list and diagram at right.

2. Cut the copper pipe to length, using a tubing cutter. Place the tubing cutter over the pipe, with the cutting wheel centered over the marked line. Tighten the handle until the pipe rests on both rollers. Turn the tubing cutter one rotation to score a continuous line around the pipe. Then rotate the cutter in the other direction. After every two rotations, tighten the

A. Measure, mark, and cut the copper pipe, using a tubing cutter. Clean and flux the pipe and fittings.

B. Dry-fit the bottom assembly of the gate, and then the top assembly. Connect the two assemblies.

handle of the cutter. Remove metal burrs from the inside edge of the cut pipe, using the reaming point on the tubing cutter or a round file.

3. Sand the ends of all the pipes with emery cloth, and scour the insides of the fittings with a wire brush. Apply flux to all the mating surfaces.

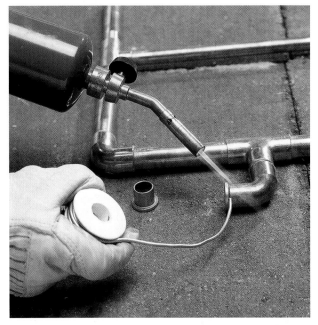

C. *Solder the joints of the gate. Add brass bushings to the latch and hinge extensions and solder them in place.*

Step B: Assemble the Gate Pieces

1. Dry-fit the pieces of the top of the gate and the display frame, referring to the diagram on page 127.

2. Assemble the bottom run of the gate, again referring to the diagram as necessary.

3. Join the top and bottom sections of the gate. Measure from one corner of the gate to the diagonally opposite corner. Repeat at the opposite corners. Adjust the pieces until these measurements are equal, which indicates that the gate is square.

Step C: Solder the Joints & Add the Bushings

1. Solder each joint, beginning at the bottom of the gate and working toward the top.

2. At each of the hinge extensions and at the latch extension, add a brass flange bearing. As you solder these bearings in place, direct the torch's flame more toward the bearing than toward the elbow—brass heats more slowly than copper.

Step D: Install & Mark the Gate Posts

1. Paint, stain, or seal the posts.

2. Mark the post positions 49½" apart on center. Dig the holes and set the posts (pages 24 to 25). As you plumb the posts, maintain the spacing between them as accurately as possible.

3. On the first post, measure and mark a point 47½" from the ground. Using a 4-ft. level, draw a line across the post at the mark, then across the opposite post. Trim off the posts along these lines, using a reciprocating saw or hand saw. Paint, stain, or seal the cut ends of the posts.

D. *Install the gate posts, then position the gate and mark the locations for the latch and for the hinge extensions.*

E. *Drill pilot holes at the marked locations on the hinge side post. Drive a lag screwhinge into each pilot hole. Make sure the hinge pin is facing up when the screwhinge is in position.*

4. Set a deck post cap and finial on top of each post and nail it in place, using galvanized finish nails.

5. Cut two 4¼" spacers. Center the gate between the posts, resting it on the spacers. Mark the hinge-side post to indicate the locations of the hinge extensions. Mark the latch-side post to indicate the location of the latch extension.

Step E: Install the Lag Screws for the Hinges

1. At each of the marked locations on the hinge-side post, drill a ½" pilot hole approximately 2¾" into the post. Drill these holes carefully—they must be as straight as possible.

2. Drive a lag screwhinge into each pilot hole, using a locking pliers or pipe wrench to twist it into place. The hinge pin needs to be facing up when the lag screw is in its final position.

Step F: Add the Latch

1. At the marked location on the latch-side post, drill a ½" hole through the post. Again, take care to drill the hole straight through the post.

2. Cut 15 to 18" of ⅜" flexible copper. Drill a hole through the tubing, 2½" from one end. At the opposite end, form a decorative coil. Cut a 2" piece of #8 copper wire and form a decorative coil at one end.

3. Insert the latch through the hole in the latch-side post. Thread the wire through the hole in the tubing, then create a small loop below the tubing. This wire loop keeps the latch from falling out of the post.

Step G: Hang the Watering Can

1. Position the watering can within the display

TIP: SOLDERING COPPER JOINTS

To solder, hold the flame tip of a propane torch against the middle of a fitting for 4 to 5 seconds, or until the flux begins to sizzle. Heat the other side of the joint, distributing the heat evenly. Move the flame around the joint in the direction you want the solder to flow.

Quickly apply solder along both seams of the fitting, allowing the capillary action to draw the liquefied solder into the fitting. When the joint is filled, solder will begin to form droplets on the bottom of the joint. It typically takes ½" of solder wire to fill a joint in a ½" pipe.

Let the joint sit undistrubed until the solder loses its shiny color. When the joint is cool enough to touch, wipe away excess flux and solder, using a clean, dry cloth.

frame on the gate. Mark the spots where the handle and spout will meet the copper pipe; clean and flux those areas. Wrap 16-gauge copper wire around the handle of the watering can, using 6 or 8 wraps of wire to connect it to the display frame in the marked spot. Add a little more flux, then solder the handle to the frame. The flux will draw the solder into the crevices between the wire wraps to create a strong, solid joint.

2. Thread a piece of 16-gauge copper wire through a hole in the spout of the watering can. Wrap the other end of the wire around the display frame in the marked location. Flux and solder the wire wrap as described above.

F. *Drill a hole on one end of a piece of flexible copper. At the opposite end, bend a coil. Insert the tubing through a hole in the latch-side post, and thread a loop of wire through the hole in the tubing.*

G. *Set the watering can into position and secure it, using 16-gauge wire. Solder the wrapped wire to the gate frame.*

Arched Gate

With its height and strategically placed opening, this gate is a great choice for maintaining privacy and enhancing security with style. No ordinary "peephole," the decorative wrought iron provides a stunning accent and gives you the opportunity to see who's heading your way or passing by. The arch of the gate also adds contrast to the fence line and draws attention to the entryway.

This gate is best suited to a situation where you can position it over a hard surface, such as a sidewalk or driveway. The combined weight of the lumber and the wrought iron makes for a heavy gate. To avoid sagging and to ease the gate's swing, you'll need to include a wheel on the latch side of the gate. Over a solid surface such as concrete or asphalt, the wheel will help you open and close the gate easily.

Shaping the top of the arch is a simple matter: Just enlarge the pattern provided on page 131 and trace it onto the siding. Then cut the shape, using a jig saw.

This piece of wrought iron came from a banister we found at a salvage yard. We used a reciprocating saw with a metal-cutting blade to cut it to a usable size.

TOOLS & MATERIALS

- Tape measure
- Circular saw w/ wood & metal cutting blade
- Paintbrushes & roller
- Hammer
- Chisel
- Drill
- Jig saw
- Level
- Framing square
- Spring clamps
- Caulk gun
- Salvaged piece of ornamental metal
- Paint, stain, or sealer
- Pressure-treated, cedar, or redwood lumber:
  2 × 4s, 10 ft. (3)
  1 × 4s, 8 ft. (13)
- Posterboard or cardboard
- Construction adhesive
- 1¼" galvanized deck screws
- 16d nails
- 2" galvanized deck screws
- 1½" mending plates (8)
- 2½" bolts and nuts (8)
- Gate wheel
- Hinge & latch hardware
- Gate handle
- Finish nails

HOW TO BUILD AN ARCHED GATE
Step A: Prepare the Lumber

1. Measure the opening between the gate posts and determine the finished size of your gate. (Check the packaging of your hinge and latch hardware for clearance allowances.) Compare your actual dimensions to those in the diagram below, then check the cutting list and make any necessary adjustments. Cut the lumber for the gate.

2. Paint, stain, or seal the pieces on all sides and edges. Let them dry thoroughly.

A. *Measure the gate opening and finalize the dimensions of the gate. Cut the pieces, and then paint, stain, or seal the lumber.*

B. *Set the blade depth on a circular saw to ¾". Mark the joint, then make a cut every ⅛ to ¼" in the joint area. Remove the waste material, using a hammer and chisel.*

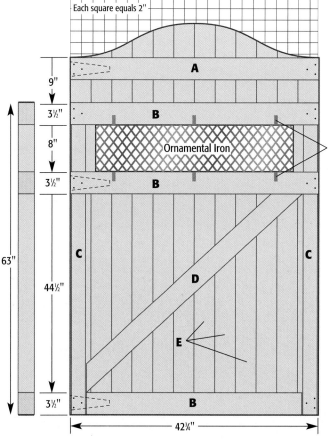

Each square equals 2"

9"

3½"

8"

Ornamental Iron

3½"

Mending plates, typ.

63"

44½"

3½"

42¾"

CUTTING LIST

Key	Part	Type	Size	Number
A	Siding brace	1 × 4	42¾"	1
B	Horizontal braces	2 × 4	42¾"	3
C	Vertical braces	2 × 4	63"	2
D	Diagonal brace	2 × 4	6 ft.	1
E	Siding	1 × 4	8 ft.	12

Step B: Build the Frame

1. Lay out the parts of the frame and mark the cutting lines for the half-lap joints (see diagram, page 131). To make a half-lap joint, set the depth of a circular saw to ¾" and cut along the marked line; make a cut approximately every ⅛ to ¼", working from the end of the board or joint area back toward that first cut. Remove the waste material and smooth the cut surface, using a hammer and chisel. Repeat with each of the marked joints.

2. Position the pieces of the frame and measure from one corner to the diagonally opposite corner. Repeat at the opposite corners. Adjust the pieces until these measurements are equal, which indicates that the frame is square. Secure each joint, using 1¼" galvanized deck screws.

Step C: Add the Diagonal Brace & Wheel

1. Position a 2 × 4 so that it runs from the bottom of the hinge side of the frame to the first horizontal brace on the latch side. Mark the angle of the cutting lines, then cut the brace to fit, using a circular saw.

2. Toenail the brace into position, using 1¼" galvanized deck screws.

3. Screw a gate wheel into the vertical support on the latch side of the frame.

Step D: Add Siding & Cut the Display Opening

1. Clamp a 2 × 4 across the bottom of the frame to act as a reference for the length of the siding. Posi-

tion the 1 × 4s even with the lower edge of the clamped 2 × 4; use 16d nails as spacers between boards. For each 1 × 4, drive three 2" galvanized deck screws at each horizontal brace.

2. Working from the back side, mark a line across the siding, 9" from the top of the gate. Run a bead of construction adhesive on one side of the siding brace; position the brace along the line and clamp it in place. When the adhesive is dry, drive two screws through each piece of siding and into the brace.

3. Starting 15" down from the top of the gate, mark an opening to fit the display piece (the opening shown here is 9¼ × 35") Use a framing square to make sure the opening is square and centered on the front of the gate.

4. Set the depth on a circular saw to ¾" (the thickness of the siding), and cut along the marked lines. Remove the siding in the cut-out area.

Step E: Shape the Top of the Gate

1. Using the grid method or a photocopier, enlarge the pattern on page 131 and transfer it to a large piece of posterboard or cardboard.

2. Cut out the shape, then trace it onto the top of the gate. Cut the siding to shape, using a jig saw.

Step F: Install the Display Piece

1. Drill three equally spaced holes across the top and bottom of the wrought iron piece. To drill into wrought iron, start with a small bit and move

C. *Position a diagonal brace from the bottom of the hinge side to the top of the first horizontal brace of the frame. Mark and cut the brace, then fasten it in place, using 1¼" galvanized deck screws.*

D. *Add the siding—use 16d nails as spacers and 2" galvanized deck screws to secure the boards to the frame. Add the siding brace, then cut out the siding in the display area (inset).*

through increasingly larger bits, drilling slowly and wearing safety goggles.

2. Set the wrought iron in place and mark corresponding holes onto the horizontal braces at the top and bottom of the cutout. Remove the wrought iron and drill a hole at each mark, drilling all the way through the frame.

3. Set the wrought iron back into position and line up the holes. For each hole, insert a bolt through a 1½" mending plate, the wrought iron and then the frame. On the back side of the gate, secure the bolts with nuts. Adjust the mending plates so they are square, then mark and drill through the siding and the frame. Install a bolt in each hole, again using nuts to secure the bolts on the back of the gate.

Step G: Hang the Gate

1. Mount the hinges on the gate. Measure and mark the hinge positions. Drill pilot holes and drive screws to secure the hinges to the gate.

2. Shim the gate into position, centered within the opening. Use a level to make sure the gate is level and plumb; test to be sure the wheel can roll freely. Mark the post to indicate the hinge screw positions, then drill pilot holes. Fasten the hinges to the post, using the screws provided with the hinge hardware.

3. Position the latch hardware on the opposite post. Mark the screw positions and drill pilot holes; drive screws to secure the latch in place.

4. Mark the catch positions on the gate. Drill pilot holes and secure the catch, using the screws provided with the hardware.

5. Install a gate handle, according to manufacturer's instructions.

F. *Drill holes through the wrought iron and the lumber, then bolt the wrought iron into place.*

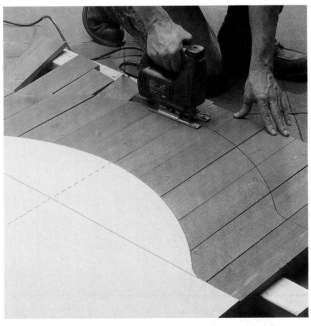

E. *Make a template and transfer the arch shape to the siding. Cut along the marked lines, using a jig saw.*

G. *Mount the hinges on the gate and shim it into position. Fasten the hinges to the post, then install the latch hardware on the gate and post.*

Trellis Gate Combination

This trellis gate combination is a grand welcome to any yard. But don't let its ornate appearance fool you—the simple components create an impression far beyond the skills and materials involved in its construction

This gate is best suited to a location where it will receive plenty of sunlight to ensure an abundant canopy of foliage. It's best to choose perennials rather than annuals, since they will produce more luxurious growth over

time. Heirloom roses are a good choice, providing a charming complement to the gate's old-fashioned look and air of elegance.

Larger, traditional styles of hardware that showcase well against the painted wood will also enhance the gate's impressive presentation. The hardware and the millwork that we used are available at most building centers, but you might want to check architectural salvage shops. They may have unique pieces that add another touch of character to the piece.

As with most of our projects, you can alter the dimensions of this project to fit an existing opening. Just recalculate the materials and cutting lists, and make sure you have enough lumber to accommodate the changes.

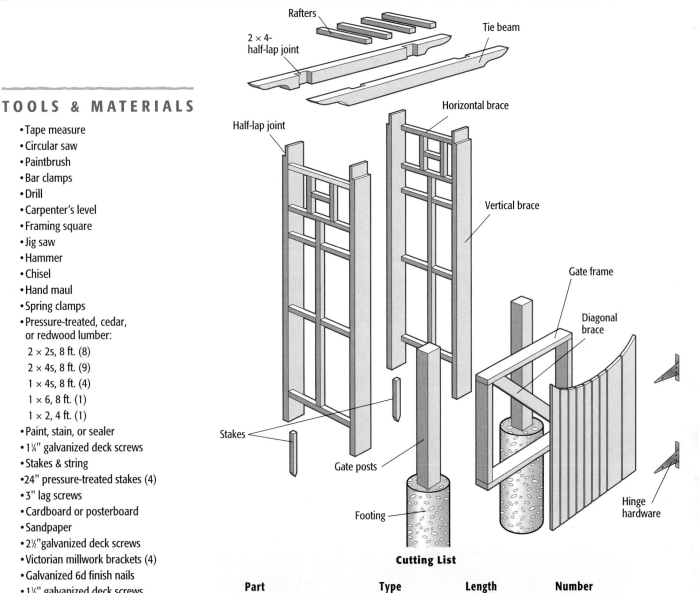

Cutting List

TOOLS & MATERIALS

- Tape measure
- Circular saw
- Paintbrush
- Bar clamps
- Drill
- Carpenter's level
- Framing square
- Jig saw
- Hammer
- Chisel
- Hand maul
- Spring clamps
- Pressure-treated, cedar, or redwood lumber:
  - 2 × 2s, 8 ft. (8)
  - 2 × 4s, 8 ft. (9)
  - 1 × 4s, 8 ft. (4)
  - 1 × 6, 8 ft. (1)
  - 1 × 2, 4 ft. (1)
- Paint, stain, or sealer
- 1¼" galvanized deck screws
- Stakes & string
- 24" pressure-treated stakes (4)
- 3" lag screws
- Cardboard or posterboard
- Sandpaper
- 2½" galvanized deck screws
- Victorian millwork brackets (4)
- Galvanized 6d finish nails
- 1½" galvanized deck screws
- Hinge hardware
- 2" galvanized deck screws
- Gate handle
- Flexible PVC pipe

Part	Type	Length	Number
Frames			
Horizontal braces	2 × 2	12"	2
	2 × 2	15¾"	8
	2 × 2	33"	6
Vertical braces	2 × 2	17"	4
	2 × 2	54½"	2
	2 × 4	87½"	4
Stop	1 × 2	46½"	1
Top			
Tie beams	2 × 4	72¾"	2
Rafters	2 × 2	33"	4
Gate			
Horizontal braces	2 × 4	40½"	2
Vertical braces	2 × 4	32¾"	2
Diagonal brace	2 × 4	49½"	1
Siding	1 × 4	45¼"	7
	1 × 6	45¼"	2

© Saxon Holt

A. *Cut and lay out the pieces for each side of the trellis frame, then secure each joint with 2½" galvanized deck screws.*

HOW TO BUILD A TRELLIS GATE
Step A: Assemble the Trellis Frames

1. Measure the opening between the gate posts and determine the finished size of your gate and trellis. Compare your dimensions to the ones in the diagram page 135, then check the cutting list and make any necessary adjustments. (The tie beams for the trellis should be about 32" longer than the width of the gate.) Cut the lumber for the trellis and gate.

2. Paint, stain, or seal the pieces on all sides and edges. Let them dry thoroughly.

3. Lay out one side of the trellis, following the diagram on page 135. Mark the cutting lines and cut the joints (for more information on lap joints, see page 131), then set the frame back together. When you're satisfied with the layout and sure the frame is square, secure the joints, using two 2½" galvanized deck screws in each joint.

4. Repeat to build the remaining trellis frame.

Step B: Anchor the Frame to the Gate Posts

1. Referring to the diagram on page 135 and to your own gate measurements, mark the positions of the trellis frame on the ground, using stakes and

B. *Position the trellis frames, clamping them against the gate posts. Attach the frame to the posts with 3" lag screws.*

C. *Square the trellis frames, then secure the free end of each frame to stakes using 3" lag bolts.*

string. Make sure the layout is square by measuring from corner to corner and adjusting the stakes until these diagonal measurements are equal.

2. Set one trellis frame into position, with the inside face of the frame flush with the inside face of the gate post. Drive a 24" pressure-treated stake behind the opposite side of the frame to hold the trellis in position. Drill three evenly spaced pilot holes through the frame and into the gate post. Attach the frame to the post, using 3" lag screws.

3. Repeat #1 and #2 to attach the other trellis frame to the opposite post.

Step C: Secure the Free Sides of the Frames

1. Check the position the free sides of the frames and measure the diagonals to ensure that the layout is square.

2. Clamp each frame to its stake and check the frame for level. Adjust as necessary. When the trellis frame is level, drill pilot holes and attach the frames to the stakes, using 3" lag screws.

Step D: Install the Tie Beams

1. Using the grid method or a photocopier, enlarge the pattern at right, and transfer it to a large piece of cardboard. Cut out the pattern, then trace the shape

onto the ends of each 2 × 4 tie beam.

12"	3½"	Variable	3½"	12"

3½"

Each square = 4"

2. Cut the beams to shape, using a jig saw. Mark and cut the lap joints as described in Step A. Sand the cut surfaces, then touch them up with paint, stain, or sealer and let them dry thoroughly.

3. Position a tie beam flush with the top of the post. Clamp the beam into place and drill pilot holes through it and into each post. Drive five 1½" galvanized deck screws into each joint to attach the tie beam to the posts.

4. Repeat #3 and #4 to install the remaining tie beam.

Step E: Attach the Rafters

Hold a 2 × 2 in position between the tie beams, flush with the tops of the beams and centered between the ends of the trellis frame. Drill pilot holes through the tie beams, one into each end of the

D. *Cut 2 × 4s, using the grid pattern, for tie beams. Dado each to accommodate the trellis frame post tops, then clamp into position and attach with five 1½" galvanized deck screws at each joint.*

E. *Attach four evenly spaced 2 × 2s between the tie beams for rafters, using 2½" galvanized deck screws.*

rafter; secure the rafter with 2½" galvanized deck screws. Repeat, placing four evenly spaced rafters across the span of the tie beams.

Step F: Add the Trim

Set a millwork bracket into place at each of the corners between the tie beams and the trellis frame posts. Drill pilot holes and secure the brackets, using finish nails.

Step G: Build the Gate Frame

1. Lay out the parts of the gate frame and measure from one corner to the diagonally opposite corner. Repeat at the opposite corners. Adjust the pieces until these measurements are equal and the frame is square. Secure each joint, using 1½" galvanized deck screws.

2. Position a 2 × 4 so that it runs from the bottom of the hinge side of the frame to the first horizontal brace on the latch side. Mark the angle of the cutting lines, then cut the brace to fit, using a circular saw. Use 2½" galvanized deck screws to secure the brace into position.

Step H: Add the Siding

1. Clamp a 2 × 4 across the bottom of the frame to act as a reference for the length of the pickets.

F. *Add millwork brackets at each corner where the tie beams and the trellis frame posts meet. Secure with finish nails.*

G. *Lay out the gate frame pieces, check for square, and secure the joints with 2½" galvanized deck screws. Mark and cut the brace, then screw it in place, using 2½" galvanized deck screws.*

H. *Clamp a 2 × 4 across the bottom of the gate frame as a guide, then attach the siding. Begin with two 1 × 6s on the hinge side, then finish with 1 × 4s. Use scraps of ⅜" plywood as spacers.*

Position the siding flush with the lower edge of the clamped 2 × 4.

2. Align the right edge of a 1 × 6 flush with the right edge of the frame. Drill pilot holes and attach the siding to the frame, using 1½" galvanized deck screws.

3. Set scraps of ⅜" plywood in place as spacers, then add a second 1 × 6. Continuing to use the ⅜" plywood as spacers, cover the remainder of the frame with 1 × 4 siding.

Step I: Hang the Gate

1. Measure and mark the hinge positions on the gate. Drill pilot holes and drive screws to secure the hinges to the gate.

2. On the handle-side post, clamp a 1 × 2 in place to act as a stop for the gate. Shim the gate into position, centered within the opening. Use a carpenter's level to make sure that the gate is level and plumb and that the stop is properly positioned. Mark the position of the stop and set the gate aside. Drill pilot holes and secure the stop to the post, using 2½" galvanized deck screws.

3. With the gate shimmed back into position, mark the hinge-side post to indicate the hinge screw locations, then drill pilot holes. Fasten the hinges to the post, using the screws provided with the hinge hardware (page 120).

Step J: Shape the Siding & Add the Gate Handle

1. Cut a piece of flexible PVC pipe 52½" long (or 12" longer than the width of your gate). Clamp the PVC at the top of the outside edges of the last piece of siding on each side of the gate.

2. Tack a nail just above the first horizontal brace of the frame at the center of the gate. If this happens to be between two pieces of siding, set a scrap behind the siding to hold the nail. Adjust the PVC until it fits just below the nail and creates a pleasing curve.

3. Trace the curve of the PVC onto the face of the siding. Remove the pipe and cut along the marked line, using a jig saw. Sand the tops of the siding and repair the finish as necessary.

4. Mark the handle location on the gate. Drill pilot holes and secure the handle, using the screws provided by the manufacturer.

I. *Clamp a 1 × 2 to the latch-side gate post and secure with 1½" galvanized deck screws.*

J. *Clamp the ends of a length of PVC pipe at each end of the gate top. Deflect the pipe down to create the curve, and trace. Cut to shape, using a jig saw.*

Contributors & Credits

MATERIALS CONTRIBUTORS

Midwest Fence
St. Paul, MN
651-451-2221
www.midwestfence.com

Minnesota Vinyl & Aluminum
Shakopee, MN
952-403-0805
www.mvas.com

PHOTOGRAPHY CONTRIBUTORS

California Redwood Association
415-382-0662
www.calredwood.com

CertainTeed EverNew
800-233-8990
www.certainteed.com

Master-Halco
562-694-5066
www.mhfence.com

PHOTOGRAPHY CREDITS

Chandoha Photography
Annandale, NJ
©Walter Chandoha: pp. 12a,
31a, 48

Crandall & Crandall
Dana Point, CA
©Crandall & Crandall: pp. 15a,
75g, 75j, 105a, 105b, 106

Firth Photobank
Shakopee, MN
©Bob Firth: pp. 3, 28-29

Saxon Holt Photography/
photobotanic.com
Novato, CA
©Saxon Holt: pp. 4-5, 113A,
117E, 134

Charles Mann Photography Inc.
Santa Fe, NM
©Charles Mann: pp.3, 6-7, 30, 31c,
44, 72-73, 74, 112a, 112b, 113b, 116

Jerry Pavia Photography Inc.
Bonners Ferry, ID
©Jerry Pavia: pp. 117a, 118a
©Joanne Pavia: Cover

Index